In my work with nearly 400 public school systems across the country, spanning a dozen years, I have witnessed and experienced a wide range of issues, hurdles, and home run ideas on the subject of family engagement. In this book, Steve Constantino brings them all—and I really mean all—together. He has woven a narrative that is at once funny and profound, anchored in research yet ready for practical implementation. Without family engagement, America's public schools risk obsolescence, and without our public schools, our democracy will lose the foundation upon which it stands. This book will inspire every educator and then arm them with step-by-step directions to revitalize our schools.

Suhail Farooqui
CEO
K12 *Insight*

Who better than Steve Constantino to offer a compelling argument to practitioners and others still skeptical about the value of partnerships between home and school? As a former teacher, high school principal, and currently as a district superintendent, Steve brings a level of practitioner credibility, honesty, and exuberance to the work of family-school partnerships that few can match. Through his telling of his own personal journey as well as his presentation of relevant case studies, activities, and reflective exercises for the reader, Steve provides us with the next go-to book on how to build and sustain effective partnerships between families and school staff that support the improvement of our schools for all children.

Karen L. Mapp, EdD
Senior Lecturer on Education
Harvard Graduate School of Education
Co-author of *Beyond the Bake Sale: The Essential Guide to Family-School Partnerships*

This is the book I always hoped that Steve would write. He tackles the thorny issues that surround family engagement with candor and courage. The stories he tells and the cases he presents are drawn from years of experience, tempered with humor and compassion. Read this book. Try out what he suggests. It will transform your school.

Anne T. Henderson
Senior Consultant, Community Organizing and Engagement
Annenberg Institute for School Reform
Co-author of *Beyond the Bake Sale: The Essential Guide to Family-School Partnerships*

In Engage Every Family, *Steve Constantino provides a simple, real-world blueprint for schools to follow that will help those schools create the welcoming atmospheres and productive partnerships that truly serve children. He is the preeminent family engagement expert because he innately understands what it takes to connect with and serve families. Steve's experience in actually implementing these successful strategies comes through in every chapter.*

Tim Sullivan
President, School Family Media
Founder & President, PTO Today

Steve Constantino takes an in-depth look at building partnerships with families—the superintendent's and the school district's most important stakeholders. This book provides an array of blueprints and other reference materials specifically targeted to foster successful relationships with the community.

Throughout my travels across the country, I encourage our members to share the great things that are happening inside their school buildings. Communities want to hear what's going on. What Steve does is help meet an administrator's individual needs when it comes to engaging with families and the communities in which they live.

Dan Domenech
Executive Director
The School Superintendents Association (AASA)

With this dynamic new book, Steve Constantino builds on his previous studies of family and community engagement. He provides an invaluable resource for educators who see the critical need to deeply involve all families as well as the broader community in the education of our children. Engage Every Family: Five Simple Principles *includes practical tools for assessing family engagement and measuring progress. An experienced teacher and building administrator who put families at the center of his work, Steve also draws on lessons learned from successful businesses. He has created a resource for treating families as customers and for generating collective impact leading to student success. I have seen his ideas in action and they work.*

Dr. Sandy Husk
Chief Executive Officer
AVID

Engage Every Family: Five Simple Principles *is a must-read for school leaders who truly value building collaborative relationships with families. Dr. Constantino provides tangible strategies that are supported by research and which ultimately lead to improved student achievement. Readers will be challenged to reflect on their own beliefs and practices and develop skills to immediately implement in their own schools. If having engaged families is a core value of yours, I highly recommend this book.*

Joe Clark, PhD
Superintendent
Nordonia Hills City School District
Northfield, OH

Engage Every Family: Five Simple Principles *provides the field with an incredibly thoughtful, comprehensive, and engaging resource that addresses what often is the major disconnect within education: Families. How to increase family engagement in the educational experience represents a major challenge to most educators, so much so that many educators often give up on engaging families in the educational experiences of their children. Before concluding that family disengagement is inevitable, educators should examine this important and powerful resource, which outlines essential ingredients for engaging families. The activities, case studies, and practical advice provided also offer readers important tools for creating an engaged culture. Finally, Dr. Constantino, a seasoned school leader, also anticipates potential areas of resistance and reluctance and provides thoughtful strategies for those educators who lean toward skepticism relative to family engagement possibilities. I highly recommend this book to all who seek to provide the strongest learning experience possible to their students.*

Dr. Spencer G. Niles
Dean and Professor
School of Education
The College of William & Mary

Family engagement is critical to any school district's success. When we are in close coordination with our parents, we have our greatest opportunity to meet the educational needs of our students.

Steve's book takes the complex issue of family engagement and provides solid and practical methods for educators to reach out to the parents in their community.

Karen K. Garza, PhD
Superintendent
Fairfax County Public Schools, Virginia

Quite simply, schools can't improve without the support and engagement of families. Steve has provided leadership at every level with practical tools to allow for the maximum engagement of families to ensure each student reaches his or her full potential. Following five simple principles, school and district leaders will begin to build upon and strengthen the unique relationship between families and schools to maximize student achievement throughout a student's educational experience.

S. Dallas Dance, PhD
Superintendent
Baltimore County Public Schools, Maryland

If you want to learn about successful strategies schools can use to engage parents, then there's no one better to talk to than Steve Constantino! We're all lucky he's taken the time to write this practical guide sharing his years of experience.

Larry Ferlazzo
Teacher, Blogger, and Author of *Building Parent Engagement in Schools*

With his new book, Engage Every Family: Five Simple Principles, *Dr. Steve Constantino has provided a valuable resource for educators, including teachers, school leaders, and support staff. By emphasizing the critical role of parent engagement in the learning process, Constantino, in an age of standardized testing, complicated evaluation programs, and nationalized curriculum efforts, reminds us that one fundamental truth remains: Families and parents matter. Strong schools do not flourish without engaged, empowered parents and families. Every school reform effort, no matter how well thought-out and backed by empirical evidence, is destined for failure without the significant involvement of families. I will highly recommend this book to our teacher educators, the teachers they prepare, and the community they collectively serve.*

Michael E. Spagna, PhD
Dean
Michael D. Eisner College of Education
California State University, Northridge

Engage Every Family: Five Simple Principles *is a must-read. It shatters the myth that many families are elusive and cannot be engaged with their children's learning. Dr. Steve Constantino, a practicing superintendent and one of the nation's leading thought leaders in family engagement, has a passion for and an expertise in this topic and takes the reader on a journey full of practical information while providing a framework, process, and prescription for success. Steve speaks directly to the reader and combines case studies, stories, ideas, and humor to motivate you to action. The time has come in education to harness the most influential teachers of students: their families. Steve Constantino will show you how to do just that.*

Dr. Paul Dulle
President and CEO
Educational Research and Development Institute

The positive impact of parental involvement in students' achievement is well-documented. Engage Every Family: Five Simple Principles *provides clear, commonsense pathways for educators to be more strategic in engaging parents and the community as partners in the education of their children. This is a must-read for teachers, administrators, and those preparing for those roles. It will assist them in creating school cultures that not only recognize and value the roles parents and community members play as partners in enhancing student achievement, but also create processes to engage and include families of students and members the community.*

Michael F. DiPaola, EdD
Chancellor Professor, The School of Education, The College of William & Mary
Chair of the Educational Policy, Planning and Leadership Department
Co-author of *Improving Instruction Through Supervision, Evaluation, and Professional Development*

In a time when education seems so complicated, leaders need books that offer simple steps that will give them the biggest bang for their buck. Where the important topic of parent engagement is concerned, this is THAT book! In Engage Every Family: Five Simple Principles, *parent engagement expert Steve Constantino provides practical steps to engage every parent in the school community.*

Peter DeWitt
Corwin author and consultant
Series editor, Connected Educators Series

Engage Every Family

Engage Every Family

Five Simple Principles

Steven M. Constantino

Foreword by Peter DeWitt

CORWIN
A SAGE Company

CORWIN
A SAGE Company

FOR INFORMATION:

Corwin

A SAGE Company

2455 Teller Road

Thousand Oaks, California 91320

(800) 233-9936

www.corwin.com

SAGE Publications Ltd.

1 Oliver's Yard

55 City Road

London, EC1Y 1SP

United Kingdom

SAGE Publications India Pvt. Ltd.

B 1/I 1 Mohan Cooperative Industrial Area

Mathura Road, New Delhi 110 044

India

SAGE Publications Asia-Pacific Pte. Ltd.

3 Church Street

#10-04 Samsung Hub

Singapore 049483

Executive Editor: Arnis Burvikovs

Senior Associate Editor: Desirée A. Bartlett

Editorial Assistant: Andrew Olson

Production Editor: Cassandra Margaret Seibel

Copy Editor: Karin Rathert

Typesetter: Hurix Systems Private Ltd.

Proofreader: Annie Lubinsky

Indexer: Jean Casalegno

Cover Designer: Michael Dubowe

Marketing Manager: Jill Margulies

Printed in Canada.

Library of Congress Cataloging-in-Publication Data

Names: Constantino, Steven M., 1958- author.

Title: Engage every family : five simple principles / Steven M. Constantino.

Description: Thousand Oaks, California : Corwin, a SAGE Company, [2016] | Includes bibliographical references and index.

Identifiers: LCCN 2015029430 | ISBN 9781506303994 (pbk. : alk. paper)

Subjects: LCSH: Home and school—United States. | Teachers and community—United States. | Parent-teacher relationships—United States. | Communication in education—United States. | School children—Family relationships—United States. | Education—Parent participation—United States.

Classification: LCC LC225.3 .C654 2016 | DDC 371.19/2—dc23 LC record available at http://lccn.loc.gov/2015029430

This book is printed on acid-free paper.

MIX
Paper from
responsible sources
FSC® C004071

15 16 17 18 19 10 9 8 7 6 5 4 3 2 1

DISCLAIMER: This book may direct you to access third-party content via Web links, QR codes, or other scannable technologies, which are provided for your reference by the author. Corwin makes no guarantee that such third-party content will be available for your use and encourages you to review the terms and conditions of such third-party content. Corwin takes no responsibility and assumes no liability for your use of any third-party content, nor does Corwin approve, sponsor, endorse, verify, or certify such third-party content.

Contents

Additional resources available at
www.drsteveconstantino.com.

Foreword

No matter how old we get, our K–12 experiences stay with us. School has a profound impact on students to the point that they remember it with fondness or regret as they move into adulthood, and just because they leave us after graduating from high school doesn't mean we will not see them sometime in the future, because most of them come back as parents. If they had a positive experience when they were students, they will most likely enter our school doors with an optimistic view of what their own children will experience as students.

Unfortunately, if they had a negative experience when they were students, they have a better chance of entering our doors with a pessimistic view and may ultimately share that pessimistic view with their children. What we do as teachers and school leaders matters, because our actions and reactions can set a negative course for our future. This history complicates the relationship a school leader or teacher may have with a percentage of their parents.

What compounds the issue even more is when schools hold up one hand inviting parents in for special events like parent-teacher conferences, open houses, sporting events, and music concerts but hold up the other hand to stop them from entering when those same parents want to discuss tough issues. In *The 7 Habits of Highly Effective People*, the late Stephen Covey wrote about emotional bank accounts. Emotional bank accounts are a part of every relationship we have, whether they are professional or personal, and they involve days where we make deposits because of positive interactions and days we make withdrawals because of negative interactions. Such is the relationship between parents and the school system. And this is where Steve Constantino enters in the equation.

Truth be told, I have been a fan of Steve for a few years now. He was one of the first educators to write a guest post for my *Finding Common Ground* blog (Education Week), and when I needed information about how to engage parents, Steve was one of the first people I looked to. In *Engage Every Family: Five Simple Principles*, Steve shows readers how they can have more positive relationships with their parents. But he also does much more than that, because he shows us how we can engage with our parents to a much deeper level than we have done in the past.

Make no mistake, we need to do more to engage parents and try our best not to send them mixed messages that leave them feeling as though we don't value their input. Schools need to be different than they have been in the past—where school is one domain and home is the other, and those two domains never mix. We all need to be more visible or transparent in our approach, but we also need to go deeper, where we ask for feedback and change some of our practices because of that feedback.

Steve Constantino's expertise is so important. Steve has not only spent his career talking and writing about the importance of family engagement, he has shown us how to do it by modeling what he wants to see. He is more than just a researcher, because he is an actual practitioner. He has been a teacher, building administrator, and central office administrator. Presently, as a superintendent, Steve works hard to bring parents into the school system, and he focuses on how stakeholders in the school can engage in real dialog. *Engage Every Family: Five Simple Principles* is an important read for teachers, school leaders, and parents because it provides five simple steps to show how they can build a stronger school community. In these times of increased mandates and accountability, we need parent support more than ever.

Peter DeWitt, EdD
Finding Common Ground blog (Education Week)
Corwin Author/Consultant
Former School Teacher & Principal

Preface

Education is a conversation, not a transfusion.

—Sir Ken Robinson

If we as educators could successfully teach all children by ourselves, then it seems to me we would have already done so. The fact that we haven't should be all the motivation or evidence we need that engaging every family in the educational life of his or her child is essential to desired school outcomes. Why haven't we been more successful in engaging every family in the educational lives of their children? Why do so many of us still struggle with the notion of engaging every family as a viable conduit to improved student learning outcomes?

Daunting questions.

I have been at this family engagement business for a long time, traveling the country and to different parts of the world sharing the message of family engagement and its powerful effects upon student achievement. Over these many years, I have had countless conversations about families and their role in education and, more importantly, how educators can better engage every family.

This book is a continuation of those conversations.

Engage Every Family: Five Simple Principles clearly outlines a pathway and process for any educator or group of educators to engage every family in the academic lives of children and acts as a framework for implementing best practices to increase the likelihood of engaging every family, including those families that have been traditionally disengaged or disenfranchised from schools.

WHAT ARE THE FIVE SIMPLE PRINCIPLES?

The book will share in great detail the logic model of the Five Simple Principles and devotes entire chapters to each of them. Below is a brief overview of the principles and why they are important in the overall scheme of connecting family engagement to learning.

1. **Principle #1: A Culture That Engages Every Family**

More often than not, desired change in an organization is often temporary, sporadic, or fleeting. This happens because the change never permeates and alters the culture of the organization. Therefore, the notion of culture as the leading standard is essential for long-term success and growth.

2. **Principle #2: Communicate Effectively and Build Relationships**

Relationships with every family are absolutely essential in the consistent engagement of families from grade level to grade level and school to school. Relationships and trust are born out of distinct, meaningful, and thoughtful systems of communication that relate a value in reaching out and connecting with every family. Communication, for purposes of this principle, also includes the important concept of welcoming environments in schools.

3. **Principle #3: Empower Every Family**

In simple terms, one definition of efficacy is the power of one (or some) to produce an effect. Establishing instructional and curricular processes that are inclusive of families begins to allow families to become immersed in school learning and to enhance and support learning at home.

4. **Principle #4: Engage Every Family in Decision Making**

Every family needs a voice in certain school decisions, and school leaders must put into place mechanisms that ensure every voice will be heard. Family engagement in decision making ensures that policies, procedures, and practices have at their core a support for engaging every family.

5. **Principle #5: Engage the Greater Community**

The key to effective community engagement is to first conceptualize what that engagement should look like, with a clear delineation of desired outcomes. There are rich and deep resources in most communities; however, many schools and districts struggle in leveraging those resources.

EVERY FAMILY AND ALL CHILDREN

"How do you work with parents who don't support the school?" a principal asked me. Later in the book, we'll dive a bit deeper into the potential responses and solutions to the challenge the question presents, but in short, it starts with an examination of what we do right now and how that might need to change.

Most schools are very adept at engaging the already engaged. The key to creating family engagement that supports better learning outcomes is to ensure that there is a plan in place that engages every family; families for whom English is not a first language, ethnic and minority families,

families that are socioeconomically disadvantaged, and families of special needs students. Every family, in this case, does truly mean *every* family. And the engagement has as an outcome better achievement for children . . . *all* children.

But, there is a brutal fact that we must confront. Since we clearly understand that use of the phrase "those students" sets differing expectation levels for student learning and hence drives expectations that ultimately drive achievement gaps, why then would we label families as "those families" and use that as a determination of our ability to engage them or, perhaps worse, allow it to provide us with a perception that they do not wish to be engaged? Do we value a relationship with a family in poverty? Do we believe it's worth our time?

Because a family is a minority family or a poor family, a non-traditional family or a family with special needs children or from a different ethnic or cultural origin has nothing to do with their desire to be engaged and see their children succeed, but these factors seem to drive excuses as to why we don't engage them. It is not family circumstances that determine engagement but our response to those circumstances that will make the difference. This book has a clear premise: to engage every family . . . period.

CONFRONTING THE NEMESIS OF SKEPTICISM

Too often in education, exposure to new ideas and initiatives has been a ritual of annual staff back-to-school meetings. Educators, especially teachers, have become suspect of most "new ideas" and even more skeptical of the annual unveiling of "this year's initiatives" by school leadership. They have seen these ideas come and go, with significant monies being spent and little change in student outcomes.

Family engagement practices are not immune from this skepticism, which is often a significant reason for lack of success with the practice. More so than skepticism is the perception of educators that strategies and efforts to engage every family are futile, largely because of apathy on the part of disengaged families. While there are many challenges to successful family engagement practices, family apathy toward their child's education is rarely one of them.

Engage Every Family: Five Simple Principles confronts the belief of educators who might not think there is value in engaging every family. Too many books start with the assumption that educators value family engagement and are just looking for ways to improve it. Other books provide research as a way to "prove" to educators that the concept is viable. Both of these options are important contributions to the body of work but dangerous in their assumptions.

This work is a conversation about family engagement, not an intravenous drip of facts and strategies. It may very well challenge the conventional wisdom of other books, but at the same time, it offers suggestions on how educators can move forward. This book encourages educators to explore, reflect, and discuss their present ideas, attitudes, assumptions, and beliefs about family engagement *before any ideas or strategies are presented*.

WHY A FIELD BOOK?

Educators have commented about the need for a working and teaching resource. Providing questions, topics for discussion, activities, case studies, and opportunities for professional reflection will link *Engage Every Family: Five Simple Principles* directly to the experiences of all educators.

Given the constraints on your time, it will be attractive to read through this book and skip over the various activities that are included. You are encouraged to not only read but also delve into the activities and reflections that are provided. To ensure that your school is successful with family engagement, try some or all of the following activities:

- Record your thoughts, ideas, and experiences as you use the book, to enhance the degree to which every family is engaged with their children's learning. Fold the corners of pages over and write in the margins.
- If you are working with a group, start a Google Hangout and keep a conversation going. Or better yet, visit **www.drsteveconstantino .com** and become part of the community that seeks to engage every family. Communicate, converse, collaborate, and reflect on the ideas presented. Have conversations with your colleagues about what you are reading and thinking. It's the best way to apply the ideas presented to your own experiences and set of circumstances. If the work is meaningful and relevant to you as an educator, then the likelihood of it having lasting positive effects are greater.
- Work with groups of colleagues to get a better understanding of the concepts presented and a better understanding of why the effort to engage every family is worth it. Discuss your ideas, your fears, and your dreams with your colleagues.
- Work together to try out new strategies and support each other's efforts. Listen to the thoughts and opinions of others and juxtapose them against your own. This type of collaboration will ensure that great things will occur.

SPECIAL FEATURES THAT WILL HELP YOU ALONG YOUR JOURNEY

Case Studies. Throughout the book there are case studies of situations that are similar to those that occur every day in our schools. The case studies include questions for discussion and reflection.

Forms, Checklists, and Needs Assessments. Where appropriate, checklists, forms, needs assessments, and other items have been included to assist you as you work through the Five Simple Principles and consider the implementation of the ideas presented.

Scenarios, Questions, and Points to Ponder. The key to this book is to reflect on present practices and, using the framework and ideas presented, create a new culture inclusive of engaging every family. To that end, there are numerous opportunities for you to respond to short scenarios, answer questions, and ponder in more depth some more of the lofty issues we face in education and how family engagement can enhance our practice.

Process Ideas. Family engagement is more a process and less a string of events to which families can attend. When appropriate, there are sections, questions, and activities devoted to the important notion of process for rich and lasting family engagement.

Where Are You? From time to time, the book will afford you the opportunity to answer the simple question: Where are you? This usually leads to a better understanding of the present situation and clarifies a path toward a desired outcome.

Graphics and Activities. Throughout the book there are activities in which you and colleagues can engage to support your efforts in engaging every family. Graphics are used to illustrate ideas and allow you to collect information and data about your efforts.

No one book can provide all of the answers and strategies regarding effective family engagement. With that said, this book makes an important point: *Strategies without process and culture change are simply ineffective or short lived.* Let's face it: If family engagement were as simple as implementing lists of strategies, it seems that every family would already be engaged.

A cookie-cutter, one-size-fits-all approach to family engagement will ensure that success remains elusive. The ideas and thoughts that *you* create coupled with the suggestions and information provided act as a foundation through which the Five Simple Principles can be implemented and measured.

WEB SUPPORT

All of the forms, ideas, checklists, surveys, and so forth will be available to you for download at www.drsteveconstantino.com. The vision is to create a large learning community immersed in the topic. Blogs, discussion boards, documents, and information is available to you by visiting the site . . . all for free. As the book and readers evolve, we hope to expand the website consistent with the needs and desires of educators who wish to engage every family. Visit the website and let us know how we can continue to support your efforts in engaging every family.

WHAT YOU WILL GET FROM THIS BOOK

There is a return on the investment of your time and energy reading this book and working through the various activities:

- You will determine the existing culture of your school with regard to family engagement and how you can help change it to be inclusive of every family.
- You will have a deep understanding of the processes and components to truly engage every family in the academic lives of their children, which will result in improved learning outcomes for all.
- You will have the chance to learn, think, reflect, and practice before you implement ideas in your classroom, school, or district. There are numerous activities, questions, and case studies to engage your thinking and actions.
- You will get ongoing website support (www.drsteveconstantino .com) with forms, ideas, checklists, surveys, and assessments, and you will benefit from the ideas of others as well.
- You will have all of the tools and resources to engage every family!
- You will see results.

AS THE JOURNEY BEGINS

Family engagement is not a cure-all, not a panacea for everything that ails our system of education, nor is it the sole solution to our student achievement woes. However, what is clear is that it will move us closer, much closer, to our goal of excellence for every student. Family engagement is a means to an end, a process that results in improved outcomes for all students.

Families who build strong efficacy with the educational lives of their children can make a huge difference in the degree to which their children are successful in school. The concept of family engagement is simple: Involve families in the learning lives of their children, and they become partners and advocates of success.

While the concept may be simple, actually making it happen can be a bit more complicated. This complication could be why we haven't seen more universal or consistent success with engaging every family. Some families, sure. Most families, sometimes. Every family . . . hardly ever. What then does it take to engage every family? It is this question that motivates this book.

Engage Every Family: Five Simple Principles is born out of necessity. Educators are strapped for time and money. We are under pressure to perform and have been conditioned to try just about anything to help our students pass the test upon which they (and we) will be graded. We must show developmental growth and mastery of learning, and we must do so with conditions that are rather dire. And, we must do so now!

Family engagement is not a quick fix. It is not a strategy that we can slap onto the school and expect to see immediate success. It is not a computer program in front of which we can plop students (or their families) for a period of time and pronounce them engaged and successful. Strategies without process *always* fail. Always.

There is no "one size fits all" portion to this book, nor is there any money-back guarantee that implementing a simple set of strategies will suddenly engage every family. *Engage Every Family: Five Simple Principles* is designed to help you change the culture of your school or district and promote the conditions necessary so that families play an important role in the educational lives of their children. The principles are by no means magic. Most importantly, this process will take time and commitment.

It is my sincere hope that this book is just the beginning. The catalyst to these dreams is you. At the end of the day, if this book captures the attention of educators and that attention results in a more universal commitment and ability to engage every family in the educational life of their children, then the stage will be set for greatness.

So, let's get started!

Publisher's Acknowledgments

Corwin gratefully acknowledges the contributions of the following reviewers:

Dana Leonard
Teacher
Ledford High School
Thomasville, NC

Tanna Nicely
Principal
South Knoxville Elementary School
Knoxville, TN

Pamela L. Opel
Teacher
Gulfport School District
Gulfport, MS

Margie Smagacz
Principal
Franklin Fine Arts Center
Chicago, IL

Cathern Wildey
Adjunct Professor
Nova Southeastern University
North Miami Beach, FL

About the Author

 For almost twenty years, Dr. Steven M. Constantino has captivated thousands of teachers, administrators, school board members, and business people from the United States and around the world. His keynote presentations and workshops have been featured in local, state, regional, national, and international conferences. Working as a high school principal in 1995, he stumbled across research about the effects of family engagement on student learning and was immediately convinced that this was the missing ingredient in helping all children learn.

Dr. Constantino's work quickly gained national prominence, and soon he began traveling the United States speaking and working with all types of educators, school board members, and businesses to promote sound practices in family engagement that result in increased academic achievement for all students. His natural gifts as a motivating orator coupled with his knowledge and practical experience make him one of the most sought-after speakers in the field of family engagement.

Dr. Constantino began his career as a music teacher and moved through the ranks. In addition to teacher, assistant principal, principal, deputy superintendent, and superintendent, Steve has also launched a company devoted to family engagement training, taught as a college professor, and authored three previous books on the subject as well as numerous articles and blogs.

Today, Dr. Constantino is a school superintendent in Virginia and still travels the globe bringing his unique message of family engagement as well as his practical processes to engage every family.

Activity: Think Before You Read!

Do not read this book . . . yet.

You have acquired a book about engaging families and the first thing you read from the author is "do not read this book...yet." Odd? Yes. Stay with it!

Before you read a word of this book, please reflect and answer the following questions. Discuss your thoughts with colleagues. Take the time now, before you delve into the ideas for engaging every family, to determine what your personal starting point is.

1. When you think about your career in education, what is your impression of the desire for families to be engaged in the academic lives of their children?

2. If you had to guess, over the course of your career, what percentage of families were truly engaged in the learning lives of their children?

3. Keeping the answer to Question 2 in mind, can you determine any patterns in the type of involvement or non-involvement you have experienced?

4. What do you think are the key ingredients to successfully engage every family in the academic lives of their children?

5. Given your answer to Question 4, how do you think you, your colleagues, your school, or your district should go about acquiring the key ingredients for success?

Answer, reflect, and discuss these questions. Then, start reading.

(Continued)

(Continued)

Record your thoughts and ideas from the questions posted on the previous page here. As you read through this book, come back and reflect on what you wrote. Taking the time to record your thoughts and referring back to them will help you in your own process of seeing how your thinking may change as you work through this book.

1

Would Every Family Choose You?

CUSTOMERS MAKE PAYDAYS POSSIBLE

I began my career as a band director and enjoyed every minute of my time teaching and making music with students. As a teacher through music, I taught an elective class. Students were not required to take my class and, if it didn't meet their needs or if their interests took them in different directions, they would drop my class. I learned very quickly that recruitment and retention was my key to success. As a former superintendent once said to me, "Remember, Mr. Constantino, customers make paydays possible."

A free, public education, for the most part, has always been the only plausible option for most families for a long, long time and is a cornerstone of our democratic society. Every child has a right to an education, and the vast majority of us have taken advantage of this right. Alternatives have always existed, but the percentage of families who would or could take advantage of these options was a small minority.

That is all changing.

There is some debate as to whether or not public education is a right of citizens, good for society, or has simply become a broken idea. Of late, others promote that education is now a commodity. While there is no direct payment for public school services, there is still payment, both in dollars and in societal good, by everyone. With a slight stretch of the definition of commodity, it could fit quite well given the direct competition to public education and the growing number of options open to families with regard to educating their children.

Public education is but one of a number of options open to families who no longer make assumptions or automatically enroll their students in public schools just because they live in a particular neighborhood. The concept of educational options to families is not a new one, but the availability of these options to a wider range of families is. With the advent of online learning options, the landscape of educational choices is changing, and it is changing quite rapidly.

In my second book, *Engaging All Families*: *Creating a Positive School Culture by Putting Research into Practice* (2003), I borrowed an idea from a wonderful book entitled *Raising Self-Reliant Children in a Self-Indulgent World*, by authors Glenn and Nelsen (1988). In their book, they argue that every parent wants their children to exceed them in their quality of life. Given the complex world in which we live and the financial realities of a postrecession economic society, most families instinctively fear that this will not occur. As a result, they are driven to help their children prosper any way they can, and for many, the path is the best education available to them.

Activity: Reflecting on Why

There is a difficult albeit important question that every educator must ask themselves: If families truly have a choice as to where their children will receive an education, will they choose our school district? Our school? My classroom? If your answer to this question is unequivocally yes, then you must ask yourself the logical follow-up question: Why? Why would families choose your school? Why would families choose your classroom or you as a teacher? What is it that is so compelling about your product that a customer will choose it over the growing list of options?

It might be difficult to think of providing an education as a product or service, and it might be more difficult to consider it as an option in an ever-crowded marketplace. Some educators scoff at the idea that education is a business and that we serve customers. There is not enough space here to continue the debate as to whether students are customers or products; both or neither . . . I've heard it argued just about every way.

When I suggest that we need to learn better customer service in education, I sometimes am plastered with sentiment that suggests my audience does not agree. More often than not, thank goodness, we inherently understand that customer service is a cornerstone of our continued successful existence. Family engagement and customer service go hand in hand.

I often challenge schools and districts to consider the first questions about choice. Then I challenge them to consider taking an action that could very well send a powerful message to families that not only do we care about their children, but we understand there are choices and we are grateful for their choice of our product.

An Idea: We Appreciate You—
A Way to Set the Stage to Engage Every Family

If you are looking for a quick way to build trusting relationships, consider this one.

Anybody who flies a great deal listens to endless announcements on aircraft before they take off, as they fly, and as they land and taxi to the gate. In the myriad of announcements there is always one that goes something like this: *"We know you have a choice in airlines and we appreciate your choosing us. We hope you will continue to choose our airline in the future."*

I have listened to an iteration of this statement more times than I can count. Interestingly, even though I have had more than my fair share of delayed and cancelled flights, postponements, and cancellations due to mechanical maladies and other types of issues that cause mayhem in my travel, I stay loyal to one particular airline. Why? Why when I have so many choices do I continue to support the airline with which I have been affiliated? Is it convenience? Do I want the air miles that much? Am I on a quest to finally get upgraded to first class? Or do I believe at some level that this particular airline truly *values* me as a customer?

My preferred airline stays in constant communication with me before, during, and after a trip. They want to know my experiences and every time . . . *every time* . . . I have responded with a concern, I have received a response. That's impressive. Even more impressive is their communication when they know a problem has occurred and they want feedback as to how they have handled the situation. They even monitor Facebook and Twitter for customer dissatisfaction and respond accordingly.

What if we apply this idea to *our* business? At some point, ask every employee of a school district, from the superintendent through the teachers to the support staff, to choose one family at random and call them on the phone. When they answer, simply say:

"Hi, my name is _____ and I am calling from _____ school (district). I just wanted to take a minute to thank you for choosing our district/school to educate your children. We know you have a choice in how to educate your child/children, and we appreciate your choosing us. We consider working with your children and your family a privilege."

Don't say another word. Just listen. Think about the responses you get.

That's it. That's the whole purpose of the message. You simply want your customer to know that you value their decision to use your product/service. Consider for a moment what would occur if every family in your school or district received this call. There would be an exponential increase in relationships and trust.

Every person who makes a phone call like this from your school district should report his or her experience. Was the message received positively? Negatively? As a result of the phone call did we learn anything about the student

(Continued)

(Continued)

or their family that will help us? How can we modify our service to meet the needs of our families in a better manner?

These are all important questions that lead to the ideal of engaging every family. What do you think would happen? What kind of responses do you think you would get? What message will families take away from this simple effort? You won't know unless you try it.

Let me know what happens. We will create a "We Appreciate You" section for you on www.drsteveconstantino.com to record and share your experiences with others. Try the idea presented and let us know what happened!

EVERY OPPORTUNITY IS A MARKETING OPPORTUNITY

Consider for a moment a world-famous soda pop company. If I shared the name with you it would be instantly recognizable. The name of this company and their brand are listed as one of the most recognizable products on the PLANET. That is saying something!

My dear friend and family engagement researcher and expert Dr. Karen Mapp often shares a story about this company and how they would pay handsomely to have audiences like the ones we get at school events. It would be their marketing dream to work with a captive audience to sell their product or elicit feedback about their product. Yet, we do little to market or elicit feedback for our product when we have these gatherings of families.

When we have families together and listening to us, we should take that opportunity to sell our product to them and explain the meaning and relevance of their child's education to them. We also need to create a culture that helps families share their feedback in a manner they perceive to be both safe and constructive. Maybe we should begin to think of these gatherings as sales opportunities?

If public education is indeed a commodity, then the concept of attracting and retaining customers is not that farfetched. If you do not believe in the commodity idea, then there is still no harm in helping every family understand why you are the best.

SOME IDEAS TO GET STARTED

The most difficult part of any experience is actually making the decision to begin. All of us have made commitments to making changes that often fall short. On New Year's Eve many of us resolve to bring a renewed energy and focus to goals in the coming year that have previously eluded us. Sometimes we follow through, sometimes we don't.

The fact that you have this book and you are still reading is some indication you are ready to start or enhance your efforts to engage every family. It seems appropriate to give you a few things to keep in mind as you get into *Engage Every Family: Five Simple Principles*. Over the years and with mountains of feedback from educators everywhere, a few common themes have emerged. They appear below as a way to draw a starting line and can act as guidelines for you as you begin your venture toward engaging every family.

Keep It Simple

We as educators sometimes tend to overthink issues, sometimes to the point of paralysis—we think that change is not worth the time or will not produce the result. We take challenges that we face and often make the avenues toward potential solutions so complex that resolving the issue seems impossible. We overwhelm ourselves with problems and ultimately become frustrated.

Simply put, we lose hope. We lose hope that we have the energy or power to change anything. We lose hope that things will change regardless of what we do. Let's commit to breaking that cycle. While I would agree with the idea that hope is not a concrete strategy, I would also argue that it is essential to improving organizations. Be sure, however, that hope is not your only strategy.

So, let's keep it simple. Simple translates into more effective action. Breaking down complex ideas into simple ones allows educators with finite amounts of time and resources to actually think and implement the ideas that are presented. Family engagement is not a race. Implementing strategies without the necessary processes and learning will result in little change to your school, or at best, temporary or sporadic change.

You do not have to read this book in a week. As a matter of fact, the longer it takes you to get through the book (assuming you are fully participating in the questions and ideas presented), the more likely your perceptions and actions are changing. As they change, so changes the culture of your school.

Engage Every Family: Five Simple Principles is designed to be simple—simple to discuss, simple to plan, and simple to execute. There are no herculean efforts needed or large budget expenditures encumbered to engage every family. As a matter of fact, engaging families is just about budget neutral. Imagine that—a way to increase student achievement that is just about free. Worth considering, don't you think?

Simple ideas presented by groups of educators supporting each other almost always results in success . . . sooner or later. Whether it takes a week, a month, or five years, so what? Measurable progress toward a goal is key. Breaking down the progress into simple, logical steps will keep the notion of family engagement very doable in the minds of just about everybody.

Remember the classic question: How do you eat an elephant?

One piece at a time. Do not expect that by implementing ideas learned in this book suddenly or magically every family will be engaged. Consider that we want to engage families, especially those that are disengaged from us, one family at a time.

Time and Patience

We are conditioned to fix everything now, today, this minute. There is no time to think, to explore, to investigate, to research, to pilot, and to assess. Because of the performance pressures placed on schools and educators, we have become a group of people wandering around akin to educational zombies looking for a quick fix to what ails us. Professional athletes spend 90% of their time training and 10% of their time performing. For educators, it is exactly opposite. That's a problem.

There are no quick fixes to the significant challenges we face in education. If there were, we wouldn't have the challenges. The necessary investment to engage every family is one of time and patience. There is no magic wand to wave that will suddenly engage the disengaged or miraculously engage every family by the beginning of the next school year. The process is often a slow one.

The best way to engage every family might very well be one family at a time. In one case, a preschool teacher worked with a family for over a year before the comfort level rose to the point where a relationship could be established.

Having patience with families, especially those that have been traditionally disengaged or disenfranchised from our schools, will unquestionably support any effort to reaffirm a commitment to their engagement. Families that are disadvantaged, families for whom English is not a first language, and families whose own school experiences were less than positive all play a role in engagement decisions. These challenges can be overcome. It just takes time and patience.

It is equally important to have patience with educational colleagues who may not see the value in engaging every family. Educators have been made a lot of promises over the years, and many of those promises never materialize. Teachers have become skeptical of educational initiatives, maybe rightfully so. Think of it this way: Family engagement is not an initiative, nor is it a new task set in front of you. Consider it doing what we already do but doing it differently, through the lens of *engaged* families—no new time commitment, no new resources, no new energies, just doing what we already do . . . differently. Don't think outside the box . . . blow the box up! Rebuild and reassemble the pieces in a different way.

Not More, Just Different

As a teacher, I remember attending the new school year opening meetings and listening to the leadership share the initiatives for the upcoming year. Over time, the word *initiative* struck fear in my heart. It usually meant that I was going to have to do something else, something new, something for which I may not appreciate the value. I learned to shudder at the word *initiative*.

Family engagement is not an initiative, nor is it a race. Family engagement is a commitment to change school culture and, as such, is ongoing and neverending. It is important to keep in mind that not everyone on a school staff or in a school district will suddenly think the notion of engaging families is a great idea. In some cases, there will likely be strong opposition to the idea—even flat-out refusal.

Consider that the implementation of family engagement philosophies, strategies, and practices are not adding new responsibilities to your already full plate. Family engagement takes into consideration what we already do; it just requires us to act differently—no new time, no new energy, no new resources—just a remolding of what we already have. To engage families means to look at our practices and procedures through a different lens—the lens of families.

During my years as a teacher and building administrator, I marveled at the sharing of ideas and resources between teachers. When one would get a good idea, others would watch to see the results. If the results were good, they would ask the originator of the idea for the information so they too could replicate the success. Great methodology is passed between teachers every day. (We'll delve into this idea a bit deeper in the next chapter.)

Educators, like the students we teach, are discoverers of knowledge. When presented with good, solid ideas that they see have positive effects on their jobs, the likelihood of their involvement and support of new ideas grows. Engaging every family and promoting the appropriate culture in a school to engage every family takes time and patience. Be encouraging, nurturing, patient, and steadfast. The results will come.

Points to Ponder

1. Discuss with your colleagues the time you devoted to implementing a new idea and the amount of time you engaged with the idea before you decided to abandon it.

2. Discuss with your colleagues those ideas and strategies that have proven effective. How long did it take to implement and perfect the ideas/strategies before you saw the success you wanted?

3. What role did the amount of time devoted to the new concept play in its ultimate success or failure?

We Already Tried That

It is the rare workshop where I offer more than a handful of new ideas to help engage every family. Quite honestly, schools across the country have captured a plethora of ideas and tailored them to their schools and specific situations. I remember one workshop participant a few years ago who said to me, "Yeah, we did the letter and the phone call and the visit and the food and the child care and the transportation and three people showed up."

I readily acknowledge that while we continue to find new ways to engage families, especially with technology and social media, most of the great ideas are out there and have had varying levels of success. So what is the answer?

It might be time to consider why your efforts, if they were marginally successful, paid so little dividend. Maybe it was the structure or timing of what you did. Perhaps the content didn't resonate with families. Maybe it was the school location that kept families away. Most likely though, the answer lies in the culture that permeates your school. Does everyone value the engagement of every family? How is that value communicated? How do we respond to situations where families do not act as we had hoped with regard to school engagement? What is our response to disengagement? Was the message of your meeting or event meaningful or relevant to families?

Make sure you understand this important fact: No one event or first attempt at engaging every family will bring a thundering herd of families to your doorway. More often than not in communities where family engagement is traditionally low, the successes are small—one family, followed by a few more families, and so forth. If you repeat an event and you increase attendance from three to five people, celebrate that! Don't be discouraged that there were not twenty or thirty people at the event. For many years I have used this adage: We engage families one family at a time. With time, we hit a tipping point, and sometimes it takes a while. Hang in there.

There is another idea about engagement that needs to be discussed. Most of the engagement that impacts student learning happens in homes away from school. I often refer to this as "invisible engagement," engagement you may not see but of which you will see the results. This is not to say that workshops and efforts to engage families are fruitless and should be discontinued—quite the contrary. The work we do outside of the home will help promote the efficacy of families when they are with their children and we are not.

In workshops, I usually give the following example of practices that I have witnessed in many schools (including my own!): School staff works tirelessly to create an opportunity for family engagement. They follow all of the appropriate procedures to be an open, welcoming environment and have practiced significant outreach to families. A central idea in the preparation of these events is the notion of its importance. We tend to drive the point home to families about how important it is that they do whatever it is we want them to do. (Come to a meeting, participate in a workshop, etc.)

When the event occurs and the family attendance is disappointing, it's not what we do next but rather more about what we don't do. We usually are exhausted from our efforts and frustrated with the results. We sulk away and vow never to expend that amount of energy again. We convince ourselves that families are simply apathetic and our efforts are a waste of time and energy. What we almost never do is follow up with our customer and find out why they didn't attend.

Consider this: If we repeatedly hammer into a family's head that taking a particular action is important and, upon their not taking the desired action we never say another word, what message have we sent? Exactly! Reinforced in the mind of the parent or family member is the idea that whatever it was, it simply was not that important. That very notion erodes trust in relationships between schools and families.

REALITY, PERCEPTIONS, AND BELIEFS

Our personal belief systems play a powerful role with regard to our desired family engagement outcomes. Families apply the very same thinking. Their personal belief systems and customs also play a large role in determining *their* level of engagement with their child's education. Understanding that perception is reality for most people underscores the need to carefully examine the belief systems of people and organizations.

When a decision is made to undertake a course to engage every family or to increase family engagement, a critical first step is to gauge where everyone is on the subject. Later in the book, ideas and activities will be presented to create a culture to engage every family. (Hopefully, you took the first step before you ever started reading this chapter.)

Can every family truly be engaged? This question has been debated over the years, and as one can imagine, the answers fall along a continuum between absolutely and absolutely not. It might be interesting to know that many urban and Title I schools have proven that 100% engagement is possible. It seems that the answer begins within one's own personal belief system.

Facts, reality, and evidence are clear: There is a strong correlation between family engagement and student learning. Every family is not engaged with their child's education. Every educator does not place the same value on building relationships with every family. Families' experiences with their children's schools shape their engagement practices over time.

Not every school welcomes families. Not every family feels welcome in their child's school. Not every family believes that their voice is heard or that their opinions or ideas matter. It will be imperative that whatever your goals in family engagement, you start with a thorough discussion and reflection on your reality, your perceptions, and your present beliefs on the topic. Not spending this time now will most likely result in very little change, if any.

The ideas below are items that should be completed before you venture into the Five Simple Principles.

Where Are You?

Directions: Have each individual member of your team or school answer the following questions independently and anonymously. Compile the answers to see where your starting point is with regard to engaging every family.

1. What do you believe about family engagement?

2. Do you believe that every family in your (classroom, team, school, etc.) is engaged with their child's learning?

3. If the answer to Question 2 is no, why do you think there are families who are not engaged?

4. If every family in your (classroom, team, school, etc.) is not engaged, would you welcome their engagement?

5. What would engaging every family look like to you?

FINALLY, THE SECRET TO SUCCESS!

Here is a story that underscores the secret to successfully engaging every family. Read through the story. The point of the story and the secret to success should be clear by the time you finish reading it.

Having numerous issues and stressors in his life, a gentleman made the difficult decision to seek professional counseling. This was a decision that did not come lightly and one that the man debated and rejected many, many times. In the final analysis, though, the man realized that without some assistance, the issues in his life would continue to affect his health and his relationships with the ones he loved. Because of this, he took the large, difficult, and scary step to seek help.

Upon arrival to the counselor's office, the gentleman was immediately put at ease. He was under no obligation to say anything he didn't want to say or take any action he didn't want to take. He was in complete control of the conversation. Almost without knowing it, an hour went by, and the gentleman was asked if he would return the following week. He agreed.

The following week (and several weeks after that) seemed to be a repeat of the first. He talked about all kinds of things, and the individual hours of conversation flew by. After several weeks, he realized he felt a bit better but really couldn't put his finger on why. At his next appointment with the counselor he decided to ask.

He walked into the meeting, sat down, and asked the counselor the question he had been pondering.

"You feel better because you have discovered the secret," the counselor said.

"The secret? The secret to what?" The gentleman was a bit irritated at the answer given to him.

"The secret to success," answered the counselor. He walked over to his desk and picked up what looked to be a picture frame and handed it to the gentlemen.

"Please read this out loud if you will," said the counselor. The gentleman looked at the frame. Inside the frame there was no picture and really no sentence or recognizable word to read. He simply saw the following:

YAGOTTAWANNA

When the gentlemen read it out loud, at that instant, he realized what the word was and what it meant.

"One's personal desire to make a difficult change starts with the very simple idea that we WANT to make the change. Without the intrinsic desire, whatever our goal, it most likely will remain elusive. You have decided to make the change. Therefore, you are." The counselor sat back waiting for a response.

"Yagottawanna, eh?" said the gentleman. "That simple?"

"That simple." The counselor smiled and said not another word. Neither did the gentleman.

The secret to successful family engagement starts with the simple notion that we desire to engage families because we believe that doing so will have a positive impact on the children we serve.

Yagottawanna. It really is that simple.

THE IMPORTANCE OF CARING

There is no question that we have many mountains to climb with regard to reforming and improving our public schools. It seems to be a reasonable conclusion, though, that the mountain that is the easiest to climb is the one that convinces families that we care about their children. Why? Because we do care! I do not recall ever meeting educators who said they simply didn't care about the children they were teaching. Further, convincing families that we care about their children is budget neutral.

The importance of caring is best summarized by another short story. This time, two neighbors, one of whom is a teacher at the local school, are discussing a decision by one of them to move his child from the local public school to a newly organized charter school.

Tom was a staunch supporter of public schools and would be the last one to abandon them. But Tom did just that. Tom removed his children from the local public school and enrolled them in a newly opened charter school. Bill, his friend who was a teacher in the local public school, knew the risks of engaging in a conversation with Tom about his decision but ultimately could not ignore the situation.

"I must admit, you caught me by surprise with your decision about the charter school," Bill said.

"There was a big part of me that was afraid to tell you, given your career and commitment to public schools," Tom responded rather sheepishly. "I want you to know that this was not a decision that we came to lightly."

Bill asked a series of questions to determine the rationale for the decision. "What is it about the education that your kids are getting at their present school that concerns you?" Bill asked. "Or is it a safety issue? I know how much the safety of children weighs on the minds of all parents." Bill thought that if he continued to share potential reasons for the switch, the conversation would go a bit better and he would be closer to understanding the basis for Tom's decision.

"I can't say that I am unhappy with the education my kids are getting. Then again, I really can't judge whether or not what they are getting is appropriate. As far as safety goes, I am more than convinced that the principal and the staff have a good plan for security. I really don't worry about my kids when they are in school."

Bill decided to prod a bit further. "I hear all the time from parents that the lack of challenging curriculum is a real issue. Is that a problem for you?"

"Absolutely not," Tom said. "Sometimes I feel like they are overly challenged and don't have time just to be kids."

"I realize that your kids are tested to death. You do know that the charter schools may require the same kind of testing, don't you?" Bill thought for sure he would hit upon the rationale his friend used to make this decision.

"I am not happy about the testing, but I am smart enough to know that the teachers didn't create this situation. We have our government to thank for that."

Bill paused a moment, a bit confused and wondering how he got this far down the rabbit hole of questions without hitting upon the reasons for the move. "So let me see if I understand this," Bill started. "You are not unhappy with the education your children are getting and you feel the school is a safe place. You are not trying to escape testing or the laws that govern education. I have to tell you, I am at a loss for why you are moving your children. It sounds like we are doing a pretty good job." As soon as Bill heard his answer, it made perfect sense.

"No, it's none of that. It's just that I feel that the charter school will care more about my children than their present school."

Bill asked Tom to elaborate.

"I need to know that somebody cares about my kids. I never really hear anything about what goes on in school and outside of typed notes about field trips, money owed, and the need for more tissues and hand sanitizer in the classroom, I don't ever hear anything. I go to the conference every year and it's pretty much the same thing—impersonal, scripted, and irrelevant.

"I get a report card with E's and S's and really can't tell you what the heck they mean. I guess my kids are doing okay, but I don't know that they are. I don't really trust the teachers or staff to care enough about my kids to tell me the truth or, worse yet, to know if there is a problem. I always feel like teachers are put out when I do call and ask a question. I never get the feeling they really want to talk with me. I always feel like when they hang up the phone they label me a problem parent."

"Considering that your children have not yet attended the charter school, what is it about the experiences you have already had that makes you think the charter school will be different?" Bill asked, not sure if he wanted to hear the answer.

"When we called the school, the lady who answered the phone was pleasant and helpful. She asked me my name and used my name throughout our short conversation. Over and over she said how happy she was that we were considering their school. Within minutes we had an appointment to visit the school."

Playing the devil's advocate, Bill said, "What if you just ran into one friendly person who has been trained in customer service?"

"That would be one more than exists at our present school," Tom shot back. "But it wasn't just the phone call or the information or the visit. From the first phone call, I felt that we were special, that the school staff really wanted us there. What was really amazing is that within twenty-four hours, all five of the people we met, including two teachers, called us to thank us for visiting their school and once again shared their enthusiasm that we might be coming to their school. I have never had this experience in any school my kids attended."

Bill was stunned. Tom's decision to send his children to a charter school had nothing to do with the quality of education or the perception of a safe school environment but had everything to do with whether or not he perceived the staff to care about his children. It occurred to Bill at that precise moment that this was the real crisis in our educational system.

The importance of caring about the families we serve cannot be understated. For *The Principles* to truly assist you in your quest, the whole issue of caring must be discussed at the start.

Points to Ponder

1. Reflect on the conversation between friends Tom and Bill. How did it make you feel?

2. Do you think that this story, which is fiction, could actually occur?

3. Where do you think your school/district is with regard to the issue of caring?

4. What systems could have avoided Tom's decision to remove his children from the public school?

5. How do you show families that you care? What more can you do?

6. What ideas can you take away from this story and implement in your school?

Ideas to Promote Caring to Families

1. There is nothing more precious to us than someone using our name, correctly. Understand the names of your students and their families, especially if they are different because of blended families. Make every contact a personal contact by using someone's name.

2. When families visit the school, give them two name tags. Allow them to put their name on one and their child's name on the other. You will never have to ask a parent who their child is again. Allowing people to make their own name tags will help you understand how to address them in the future. It also makes life easier for teachers and staff members trying to remember names in blended families.

3. Make your first interaction with a family about them, not about you, your classroom, or the course you teach. Demonstrate your desire to learn about them, their family, customs, rituals, challenges, and so forth.

4. Whenever possible, have face-to-face conversations or at least telephone conversations. In this world of mass communication, much is lost in texts, e-mails, and 140-character messages.

5. Consider home visits (breathe . . . we'll discuss this in more detail later) to those families who are reluctant to participate.

6. When families are invited to an event, take attendance and pay close attention to those who are not there. Call them and tell them you missed them. Offer to share the information with them in another setting. Do not judge their absence or ask them why they were absent, simply reinforce that the information is important and you want to share it with them.

7. Smile. Don't allow the few negative experiences you may have had with some families to color your attitude toward others.

I bet you can think of others! Write them below:

THE IMPORTANCE OF PROCESS

Strategies without a process produce sporadic and temporary results.

Schools and districts wishing to improve their quality of experiences for staff, students, families, and communities understand that redesigning internal processes of the organization will ultimately lead to improved performance. Schools and districts will need to create processes that are self-sustaining over time and are capable of delivering the required performance objective.

We tend to make the time to create the necessary processes to attach to goals and ideas we wish to implement. We often forget the natural dips that occur in organizational effectiveness when we introduce change. Consider the following charts, which help us to understand the change process:

Figure 1.1

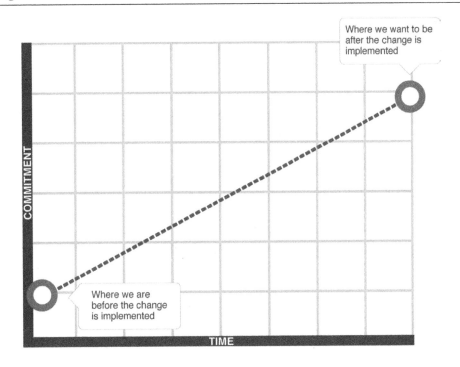

Often, when we implement a change in an organization, we believe that while there may be a few bumps in the road and a few problems to resolve, generally speaking the change will occur as depicted in the chart above; a slow but steady elevation to our desired state. Unfortunately, this is not usually the case. Change is a messy business. More often than not, it looks more like this:

Figure 1.2

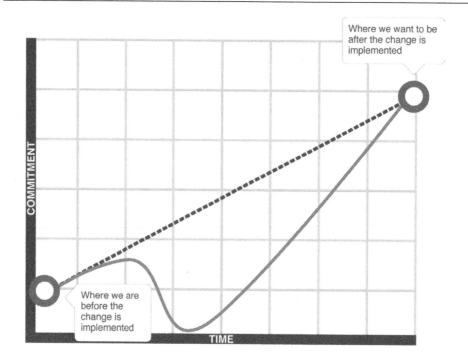

Change, in any organization, usually plunges some or all of the organization into a chaotic state. More often than not, things get confusing and frustrating before they get better. Then as the change takes hold and the despair turns to acceptance and finally advocacy for the change, the desired state is reached. None of this, however, can be done without explicit processes in place. Strategies without process do not work.

Process Exercise

Spend some time reviewing how you process change in your organization.

1. Is your organization used to developing processes that are measured and evaluated over time? If not, what do you think will have to occur in order to become "process oriented?"

2. Is the leadership of your organization truly committed to the work of family engagement? If so, how will that commitment be translated to your entire organization?

3. Are you willing to examine the culture of your organization, both positive and negative attributes, in order to bring about improvement?

THE NEED FOR LEADERSHIP

The ingredients to successfully engage every family are as specific as any favorite recipe. Regardless of how well you implement and evaluate your success, if the support of leadership is missing, the recipe will not turn out as expected. Strong, committed, courageous leadership is essential to long-term success.

Several years ago, a question was asked of me about successful family engagement programs that had been launched in schools around the country. The question was simple: Was there a commonality between those programs that were successful and those that were not? After pondering this question for a while, the answer was clear: Yes. The commonality was supportive and purposeful leadership. Superintendents and central office staff who stood up and set a vision and direction for a school district that was inclusive of families had better results. Principals and building leaders who championed the cause saw better, more consistent, and measurable results as well.

Of all of the leadership qualities one can possess, it seems courage is an absolute necessity if leaders wish to engage every family. Changing the direction of organizations and having the will to make changes that can begin as uncomfortable are essential ingredients in engaging every family. Courage comes from facing and overcoming fear. Most people in most organizations fear change. Creating the conditions to engage every family will likely be a significant departure from standard practice at your school or in your district.

In many workshops over the years, some teachers and school staff members have approached me to share two very specific ideas. First they want me to know that the concepts and information I am presenting are ones in which they believe and which they value. The second statement they make is the alarming one. Often, they tell me that they do not perceive that their leadership (district or building) places value on the topic. I have been repeatedly asked what teachers can do to convince leadership that the practice of family engagement is worthwhile and brings about better achievement. I usually try to persuade them to try the ideas and share the positive results with their leaders as an effort to try and begin to change the culture.

With these ideas and the notion that families will choose you, the sky is the limit as to your success in engaging every family.

2

A Quick Note About Motivating Teachers

There is a common theme in the conversations I have in my own school district and with teachers and administrators across the country. Teachers do not feel valued. Morale is at an all-time low. Teachers are losing momentum and are somewhat beleaguered by the constant media and political assault on public education, the demands on their time, the ever-growing set of standards that must be mastered by all students and new levels of accountability, and the ever-dwindling resources available to public education.

While I don't deny the reality and severity of these issues, I continue to see progress in student learning. More students are successful in school. In my own district, we have made progress with our students year after year. How can unmotivated, demoralized teachers produce such results? Maybe the answer lies in the degree to which teachers are or can be motivated to be their very best.

In a recent Phi Delta Kappa poll (2014) of 170,000 Americans, 10,000 of which were teachers, teaching was found to be the second most satisfying profession after medicine. The same poll found that in contrast to their overall happiness with their jobs, teachers often rate last or close to the bottom for workplace engagement and happiness.

Bolman and Deal (2002) articulate the challenge as the failure of "teacher proofing" reform initiatives. Pink (2009) described the three important factors for motivation in the workplace: autonomy, mastery, and purpose. It is this last notion, purpose, in which family engagement can play a huge role.

Upon entering their chosen profession, a majority of teachers have a strong sense of purpose. Administrators and families that support teachers will allow a teacher to sustain their purpose in advancing the learning of an increasingly diverse country of learners. Students connect to the person that is teaching, not simply the content being taught. Families react in much the same way. Teachers are motivated by a desire to give. Family engagement can considerably enhance this desire.

To ignore teacher motivation is to almost cast a death knell on the culture of schools and education. Later, we will learn that culture is made up of the collective beliefs, values, and assumptions of people within the organization. The degree to which people are motivated toward peak performance will go a long way to ensuring a positive and thriving organizational culture.

Research has articulated a great number of positive outcomes when efforts are made to successfully engage families in the academic lives of their children. In a study conducted by Epstein and Becker (1982), a large population of teachers were asked to share what they believed was the largest barrier to their success as a teacher. Interestingly, an overwhelming number of those teachers indicated they wished they had more support from the home for what they were trying to achieve in their classroom.

Family engagement produces a number of positive outcomes for education. One of them is clearly the improved attitudes and morale of teachers. When students do better in school, homework completion rates improve, attendance improves, and student behaviors improve, so does teacher desire and morale (Epstein et al., 2009). When families and teachers are working together, on the same page, everybody wins. This collaboration does not happen by itself. It takes a commitment to the idea, reflection of practice, and work toward building trusting relationships with every family.

It has been my honor to conduct workshops for educators for many years. More often than not, some workshop participants will confirm with me that they share the same opinions and values about engaging families but wish their superiors or others in charge felt the same way. In some cases, as unbelievable as this may sound, teachers are discouraged by their own leaders to engage families. In a workshop, one teacher told me, "My principal said that the last thing we needed were parents running around the school all day long."

A very simple step toward engaging every family is to support those educators who are already convinced that the outcomes of family engagement are worth the effort. As this grows, a tsunami of engagement will occur, and good things will start to happen. It's hard to ignore or cast dispersion over progress.

Many schools have instituted parent liaison positions. These positions, found commonly in schools receiving Title I funding, are dedicated to creating inroads with every family and bridging the gap between home and school. Used effectively, these liaison positions can create an atmosphere of trust in schools and can also serve as a vehicle to connect families with classroom teachers.

While these positions can be critical to the goal of engaging every family, it is important they not be used as substitutes for the necessary relationships between teachers and families. In some cases, these positions are used to make discipline phone calls or are asked to serve in utility capacities, such as extra help in the cafeteria, hall duty, and duties at arrival and dismissal. If these positions are relegated to these operational tasks, the desired outcome of engaging every family will be lost. Further, if they are used as substitutes for relationships between classroom teachers and families, teacher motivation can suffer.

THREE KINDS OF TEACHERS: A SLIGHTLY HUMOROUS LOOK

In almost every workshop, conference session, or question-and-answer period I invariably get this question: How do you get teacher buy-in for family engagement?

It's a great question.

I usually start the answer by sharing my opinion of the types of teachers we have in our schools. Mind you, my comments are not based in one shred of research but rather born from my experiences and observations of teachers over time. These descriptions are meant to be humorous, and while people are laughing, they usually nod their head in agreement. That affirmation I get provides me with the motivation to share with you "the three types of teachers." Every school usually has these three groups, with minor variations.

Group one is a small group of teachers I call the "happy peppy teachers." They have boundless energy, are creative, and are usually happy morning people. They are the first to offer new ideas and the first to volunteer for just about anything in the school. If there is a sunshine committee . . . these teachers are on it. If the principal asked them to run naked down the street, they are shedding clothing as they bolt out the front doors of the school! They are happy, peppy, and full of spirit, energy, and optimism. They never sleep and seem to be at school all the time. Some students believe these teachers are obviously robots and must plug themselves in somewhere to recharge.

Group two is the largest group of teachers I call "the wait-and-see-ers." This is a group that does not usually fully commit to doing anything, nor do they refuse doing anything. They simply wait and see. They wait and see if the idea presented will be around in a week or a month. They have seen ideas, practices, procedures, initiatives, and sure-fire solutions to problems come and go.

They also wait and see if the leadership desiring the action will be around in a week or a month. They have seen them come and go as well.

As a former principal of a school offering the International Baccalaureate (IB) Programme, I once had a teacher say, "I bet you didn't know I was an IB teacher?"

"No," I said, "I didn't know that."

"Yup, *I be* here when you got here and *I be* here when you gone!"

The wait-and-see-ers do just that . . . they wait and see.

Group three is usually the smallest group of them all, but they pack a powerful punch. I call them the "not-gonna-do-its." No matter what you want, they are simply not going to do it. At meetings, their arms are folded across their chest, that is, at the meetings they actually attend. They can be highly skeptical or, worse yet, negative. No matter what the idea, they will find some way to be critical. The "not-gonna-do-its" are a tough group with which to foster change in an organization.

It is often impossible for leaders to change the mindset of this last small but powerful group of people. The answer lies in changing the culture of the organization. As the genesis of a new culture of relationships and open communication is created, it forces the "not-gonna-do-its" to either conform to the new norm, or in some more drastic cases, leave the organization altogether.

This humorous look at teachers highlights the fact that in every organization there exists a wide continuum of attitudes and assumptions about change, ideas, or initiatives. However, it is important to remember one salient issue: No teacher *wants* to fail.

We have to take some responsibility with regard to the level of skepticism that exists among the teaching force. We have paraded an awful lot of things that were guaranteed to either make their lives easier or improve student learning seemingly by magic. Teachers look upon these ideas as passing fads—here today, gone tomorrow. No wonder that most of them "wait and see" if something will stick around for awhile.

CAN I GET A COPY OF THAT?

Teachers are always willing to share good, practical ideas for improving instruction and learning. Teachers also gravitate quickly to things that work. They watch each other intently, and when a colleague has success, they are quick to replicate the ideas in their own classroom. Proof-of-concept almost guarantees that most teachers will implement the desired practice or idea. In extreme circumstances, teachers have been known to "borrow" ideas and replicate them in their own classroom. However it occurs, one thing is clear: Good ideas spread among teachers.

The implementation of new ideas and change in an organization is not easy. My best advice is to find that small group of happy, peppy teachers and launch the concept. Their colleagues will watch, hidden behind walls and doors, but they will watch. Slowly but surely, the ideas will take root and over time, almost magically, concepts will permeate the culture of a school.

Forcing change that is not prescribed in law or regulation doesn't usually work very well. Teachers are also very compliant people. If you force them to do something, whether they like it or not, they will usually do it. If the change demonstrates the results and desired outcomes, teachers incorporate it into their culture. However, if the change doesn't achieve the outcomes desired, the change doesn't last very long, and before you know it, there is no change at all. While some forced change could be argued as necessary, most of this type or organizational change ends up doing nothing more than further driving motivation and morale to a deeper negative level and has the potential to damage leadership credibility. Leading change means leading *cultural* change.

Planting the seeds of ideas, nurturing those ideas, celebrating and replicating successes, and devoting organizational resources to the change are all important ingredients. This is not a book about change theory; however, when thinking about family engagement as a conduit to organizational improvement, the process of change matters.

MY DUMB IDEA

During my years as a building administrator, I launched a lot of new ideas—some good, some not so good. I remember, when I was sharing with the faculty a new piece of technology that would revolutionize communication with families, the skepticism ran high, so high in fact that one teacher wrote to me anonymously and said in part, "This is the dumbest idea I have ever heard and I have been here for over 25 years and heard a lot of dumb ideas!"

I knew that if we could implement and prove the concept, sooner or later, most teachers would engage. Three years later I got another note, presumably from the same teacher. Unsigned, the note said:

"Three years ago I told you your telephone idea was dumb. I want to say for the record that I was wrong. In fact, the ideas that you presented have helped all of us be better teachers and most importantly have helped more students be successful."

It is a mistake to ignore the role of motivation in launching a process to engage every family. Understanding the beliefs and values of people within the organization will help leaders better articulate a successful pathway.

In my opinion, the secrets to motivating teachers are simple. First, believe that teachers want to be successful. Second, understand that until we can prove a concept, skepticism will run high. Lastly, understand that when the first two conditions are met, teachers will gravitate toward the desired change. Their timeline may not be your timeline, but with nurturing, nudging, and a little patience, the results will be spectacular.

3

Understanding Disengagement

I think we too often make choices based on the safety of cynicism, and what we're led to is a life not fully lived. Cynicism is fear, and it's worse than fear—it's active disengagement.

—Ken Burns

A student is struggling in school. The teacher makes repeated attempts to contact the child's family in order to inform them of the issues. Regardless of what effort the teacher makes, there is no response. In a last ditch effort, a letter is sent to home requesting a conference. The letter goes unanswered.

Can you relate to the situation above? What is your first thought when reading it? Before you read any further, in the space below, write down what you believe about the student, the parent/family, and the teacher.

The Student:

(Continued)

(Continued)

The Parent/Family:

The Teacher:

It is logical for any educator faced with the scenario above to assume that the parent(s) or family of the student is simply apathetic toward their child's success in school. No one would blame a teacher for giving up on trying to engage seemingly apathetic parents. "There is only so much I can do," said one teacher in complete frustration.

But what if this alleged apathy wasn't apathy at all? What if there were reasons for the behaviors demonstrated by the parent? What if there was a system that could be implemented and strategies that could be employed that would not only prove the parent was not apathetic but actually improved the engagement of the parent as well? Understanding the roots of disengagement helps to reverse the trend.

Hornby (2011) suggests that parents' beliefs about involvement, parents' current life situations, parents' perceptions of the school's desire to engage them, and class, ethnicity, and gender are all factors in parent disengagement. Parents and teachers can often work from different agendas, have differing opinions and attitudes, and use different language.

Challenges to effective and meaningful family engagement exist for both schools and families. Limited resources to engage families with schools create some of the challenges. Most others, however, originate from the beliefs and perceptions of both families and school personnel (Liontos, 1992).

While there may be challenges to family engagement that are specific to specific schools, generally speaking, the most common challenges include the perception of teachers that engaging families will take more time than they can devote given the expectations they already have (Caplan, 2000). Even though many poorly educated families support learning, many teachers perceive this not to be the case and believe these families cannot help their children (Caplan, 2000).

Communication is a huge factor in disengagement. Many times school efforts to increase family engagement fail because of differing styles and types of communication between schools and families. Languages play a huge role in this problem as well. Other challenges to family engagement include lack of transportation, time, and comfort in engaging with the school. Because many parents had negative school experiences, it is often the norm that they transfer this negativity to their own engagement (Caplan, 2000; Liontos, 1992).

School can be a very unwelcoming place for many families. Whether their experiences were negative or, in the case of families with limited English proficiency, their intimidation of schools and lack of knowledge of the U.S. culture all combine to keep them from outwardly engaging with the school. There can also be points of tension and conflict between families and teachers (Baker, 2000; Caplan, 2000; Liontos, 1992).

Some families hold onto the perception that they do not have easy or thorough access to information about school. They believe that teachers blame them when their children have issues in school and feel unwelcome to engage. These same families believe that teachers only share negative information and that teachers wait until things are at a boiling point before communicating with the family.

Teachers on the other hand believe that families do not respect them or the job that they do. Teachers are concerned about decisions that are questioned and, in some cases, believe that families encourage their children to be disrespectful to the teacher. Teachers desire more support from homes for what they do in their classrooms (Drake, 2000).

Let's take a look at the following statement from a teacher:

> In my over 30 years of working with students as a teacher and administrator, I have run across all kinds of families—those that are completely uninvolved, those that are too involved, and everything in between. I have worked with students who come from rich families, poor families, immigrant families, families who are homeless, broken families, foster families, incarcerated parents, various races and ethnicities of families, and families that face crises the likes of which I could never have imagined. In all those years, with all those families, I never ever met one that didn't care about their children.

What do you think about the statement that appears above? Do you agree? Disagree? Why? How does the statement make you feel? Write down what you believe about the statement or any thoughts you have about the statement here:

Fundamentally, your success in engaging every family will come down to what you think about families, every family, and their value as partners to support student learning.

Now, let's take a look at what the late Ron Edmonds, researcher and founder of the Effective Schools Movement, said about our beliefs toward families and their children:

How many do you need to see? How many effective schools would you have to see to be persuaded of the educability of poor children? If your answer is more than one, then I submit that you have reasons of your own for preferring to believe that pupil performance derives from family background instead of school response to family background. Whether or not we will ever effectively teach the children of the poor is probably far more a matter of politics than of social science and this is as it should be.

We can, whenever and wherever we choose, successfully teach all children whose schooling is of interest to us. We already know more than we need to do that. Whether or not we do it must finally depend on how we feel about the fact that we haven't so far. (as cited in Lake Forest College, 2010)

This statement is built upon research by both academic and field researchers who came to the same conclusions: Given certain organizing and cultural characteristics found in the researched schools and their districts, all children can be taught the intended curriculum and held to high academic standards that enable students to achieve successfully at the next grade level.

So, then, the important question becomes a very tough question to ask: Do we care? That becomes the salient question when embarking on a process to engage every family. Do we truly care about every child we teach? Do we believe that there is value in all children? Do we believe that there is a benefit to children and to us by exerting effort to engage every family?

It is absolutely imperative that we examine our beliefs and the system of beliefs that drive our schools. Not taking the time to do so will bring about little change not only in family engagement but to any effort we undertake that has at its core a goal for fundamental improvement. It is possible that after close examination, the root of family disengagement could rest with us.

Disengaged people, regardless of who they are, are disengaged for a reason. The reason can be as varied as the disengaged themselves. However, we do know that people are not born disengaged but rather become disengaged. Circumstances present themselves in such a manner that disengagement from an organization or a process is determined to be the best coping option. That is the cycle we need to break.

THE CYCLE OF DISENGAGEMENT

The cycle of family disengagement from schools and education is depicted by Figure 3.1.

The model starts with the premise that people are not born disengaged but become disengaged because of circumstances in their lives.

Figure 3.1

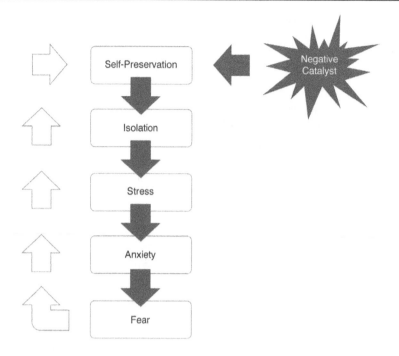

For example, in the workplace, if a new employee is demonstrating exceptional skills and has garnered the attention of his superiors, his colleagues may resent the fact that his performance is raising standards and expectations. The employee is confronted by his colleagues and as a result of this exchange, lowers his standards and productivity. This negative catalyst begins a cycle of disengagement.

In education, families can experience negative catalysts in a number of scenarios. Perhaps the assigned teacher is not the teacher a family hoped their child would work with, or perhaps they hold the perception that a child was admonished unfairly by a teacher, leader, or other staff member. Whatever the issue, a negative catalyst is the match that lights the fuse of disengagement.

When confronted with negativity and danger, most people immediately look for ways to protect themselves from the perceived threat. This process of self-preservation is a very normal response to threatening circumstances. While there are many ways one can protect themselves (you have heard the phrase "fight or flight"), the simplest way is for one to isolate themselves from the threat, negative catalyst, or perceived danger. It is at this juncture that educators should reach out and do all that is possible to avoid the self-preservation and isolation that occurs. If we don't, matters tend to get worse.

What causes stress? While there are entire books written on this one subject, I think it safe to say that the nucleus of stress are problems or challenges that are not resolved, not easily resolved, or for which there is no perceived resolution. Families in distress over issues, however large or small (negative catalysts), harbor that stress, and left unresolved, it often morphs into a form of anxiety. Believing there to be an issue with your child at school but feeling helpless or powerless to do anything about it causes stress.

As our world becomes more complicated, it seems that more and more people are anxious, with good cause. The recession, terrorism, political polarization, and so forth lead to levels of anxiety in all of us. However, some people have challenges with anxiety that are beyond what the majority of us face. They are in a perpetual state of worry. That worry, left unresolved, allows them to begin to ruminate on problems, causing them to believe things that may or may not be true.

I have explained this phenomenon in workshops by using this example.

Several years ago, a fictitious man, I'll call him Bill, suffered from generalized anxiety disorder (GAD). This disorder is characterized by exaggerated worry and tension, even when there is nothing to worry or be tense about. For example, if he hears a siren or sees an emergency vehicle speed by, his first thought is that one of his family members is hurt or in danger. He often has to contact his family by phone to provide himself reassurance that they have not fallen in harm's way. The exaggerated worry forces the phone call, and hearing the voices of his family resolves the anxiety. Most of us barely pay attention to these things, but people like Bill who suffer from GAD become very concerned about something as simple as a passing siren.

How then does this relate to family disengagement? I am certainly not suggesting in any way that families who are disengaged suffer from disorders like GAD! I only use that example to illustrate how powerful anxiety can be. Families who are anxious about their children's school experiences often become fearful of the school and fearful of speaking up. They believe that by doing so they could inadvertently bring harm to their child in the form of retaliation from school personnel. I get a lot of hands raised when I ask audience members if they have ever been the recipient of anonymous communication about their classroom, school, or district. I usually share this dialog with workshop participants and allow them to finish the conversation. I will do the same with you.

Anonymous caller: You have a problem (describes problem).

Educator: If you will give me your name and number, I will look into the matter and call you back.

Anonymous caller: Oh, I can't do that, because if I do, you will . . . (finish this statement).

Audiences for years have responded in unison ". . . take it out on my child." That's anxiety that leads to fear.

Fear then triggers a further desire to preserve oneself (or their child in this case) from danger or retaliation. As families move through this cycle, they become less likely to engage with school personnel and more likely to become disenfranchised from schools. It is this cycle of disengagement that the Five Simple Principles helps to eliminate.

This is but one of a number of examples of disengagement. Some families do not feel confident in working with the school because of their own level of education or their own experiences with school. Adult literacy remains a significant barrier for some families. Still other families feel inferior because of the barrier of language. Whatever the reason for disengagement, the important message is that with effort and knowledge disengagement can be reduced and eliminated.

WHY SOME FAMILIES STAY AWAY FROM SCHOOLS

Consider the plight of the following family.

In the last thirty days, the Jones family had been warned by two utility companies that failure to pay toward their bill would result in termination of service. Mr. Jones, who had been employed in two jobs, was now informed that because of sluggish sales he was being laid off from his second job. Mrs. Jones found work but the pay was less than what Mr. Jones made at his former job. In addition to the utilities, the Joneses were also contemplating what to do at the end of the month. It appeared that they would not have enough money to pay their rent as well.

The Jones children arrived home from school and shared with their parents the need for money for a variety of school activities with which they wanted to engage. The Joneses, not wanting to disappoint their children, simply smiled and indicated they would work something out. Unfortunately, they had no idea what they were going to do.

Is it any wonder that a family like the Jones family does not attend school functions or meetings? On any given evening, the family priorities are dominated by ensuring that their living conditions are suitable for their children. They struggle to keep the lights and heat on and food in their home. Often, the Jones children return to school with missing or incomplete homework, and they rarely participate in school events outside of the school day. The Jones family cares deeply about their children; however, they cannot engage with their children's education in a manner that we as educators would like to see.

School perspectives often make a dangerous assumption: Children do not succeed in school because their families do not support the efforts of the school to educate their child (Finders & Lewis, 1994). The assumption of apathy is one of the largest barriers to creating effective relationships with all families.

The idea that disengaged parents are apathetic toward their child's education seems to permeate the attitude of some educators and the culture of schools. We as educators tend to make a huge assumption that if one is not involved then the reason can only be apathy. This is a dangerous assumption. There are numerous reasons families stay away or are disengaged from the educational experiences of their children. In the case of Latino and other immigrant families, school experiences, economic and time constraints, language, and cultural practices are all barriers (Finders and Lewis, 1994). Often factors such as time, distance, and issues of day care are used as reasons for the lack of engagement, when in actuality the controlled nature of family-school interactions and the institutionalized nature of relationships are much more common barriers (Smrekar & Cohen-Vogel, 2001).

Gathering Information on Disengagement

Conduct a mini-research project. When families seem disengaged from their children's education, reach out and begin a dialog. Determine why families seem disengaged. Is it time? Fear? Adolescence? Perceived relevance of information? Language? Educational level of parent? As you reach out and have these crucial conversations, note the reasons for the disengagement from whatever it was you had hoped the family would engage.

Determine the percentage of parents who said "I don't care about my child."

The Five Simple Principles are designed to first illustrate why disengagement exists and then to *create a system* that begins to reverse the trends of disengagement.

These principles are not simply strategies. If we as educators do not believe that engaging every family will bring about improvements in student learning, then there is *not one* strategy that exists that will bring about the desired change. However, if we are willing to examine our own beliefs, confront the brutal facts of our present conditions, and possess both the willingness and patience to change our own destiny, then a world of ideas will be at our disposal and real change will occur.

The principles are designed so that we may reflect on our beliefs and practice as educators and then take the necessary actions to engage every family. Then and only then will change in the learning outcomes for all students become a permanent reality.

THE VERY FEW

My father was a barber for over fifty years, almost until the day he passed away. He quit school at the conclusion of the sixth grade to assist his family financially. My mother, considered by far the most educated in her family, finished high school and began a career as a secretary. Over the years and working for only one company until her retirement, she rose through the ranks to become a department supervisor. Throughout my entire upbringing and well into my adult life, my parents hammered into my head one clear unwavering message: You must get an education to succeed in this world . . . and . . . you will! There were no alternatives presented. My grandmother almost scoffed at every degree I attained, stating repeatedly at each commencement, "you have to get that doctor's degree and then you'll have something!"

Like many in their generation, my parents were the children of immigrants. Ingrained in them was the simple notion that hard work and sacrifice would provide great rewards, mainly in a better quality of life in a country where opportunity was virtually everywhere. They also believed that their efforts would allow their children access to education and that education would allow their children to succeed as well. My parents' education, though minimal, allowed them to exceed their parents' quality of life, and my education allowed me to exceed my parents'. Today, however, many families struggle to allow this generational pattern to continue. In greater numbers, our children are struggling to exceed our quality of life and it scares us.

Engaging families in the school lives of their children is essential to ensuring that all children learn to their fullest potential. I haven't met too many people who disagree with this statement, but I have met countless people who are frustrated by the challenges and obstacles of getting it done. Family structures have changed, communication style has changed, the structure of jobs and careers has changed, transiency and mobility of families have changed, and education itself has changed.

Some educators hold the belief that families simply don't care to do more (or anything) to support their children and often cite culture or economic status as a reason. Given the statistics of some student performance and the attendance rates of families to school events, it's easy to think this way. But there is an important point that can be made with regard to disengagement and our perception of it.

While there are significant percentages of families who may be disengaged with their children's learning, a very small portion of those families are driven by apathy toward their children's education. It is a poor assumption to think that, because someone is disengaged, the reason is apathy. If we consider the idea that at a minimum, 99% of families care about their children's education and want to see their children succeed and surpass them in quality of life, the opportunity to create conditions for this to happen are simply endless.

It is very common for us to believe that family interest in engaging with school has something to do with either culture or economics. While we must acknowledge differences in people and families and understand that processes to engage them may be different in different places, the principles recommended in this book are *universal* and apply to every situation. Those that disengage with organizations, more often than not, do so because they do not see the value in their participation, the meaningful nature of what that engagement might look like, or how the engagement is relevant to them. Different cultures and economic variances in families might require different strategies to engage but are clearly not a rationale to explain their disengagement.

In my travels, I have seen situations in schools and communities where the odds of success seemed hopeless. In a small town in Appalachia, for example, students aspired to follow in the footsteps of their parents and attain welfare. In many urban settings I have visited, families were all but invisible at things like school conferences or meetings designed to help families help their children or understand what was being taught and learned in school. In the rural parts of the United States, the distance from family to family and from families to schools convinced educators that trying anything to engage was simply fruitless. None of these situations are hopeless. There is a common thread between every family, that being their heartfelt desire *that their children exceed them in their quality of life.*

If we perceive that we have poor family support, we can change it. The most difficult step is the first one. We must be the catalyst in the process to build relationships and engage families. We must believe there is value in working together, building a partnership that supports every individual student and family regardless of who they are, what language they speak, or where they come from. School personnel that understand the value and dividend of reaching out to parents and families are poised to ensure that their students will succeed.

Today, even though the world is a very different and complicated place, the dreams and ideals that parents hold for their children are similar to the ideals my parents held for me. Researchers keep asking parents what is important to them, and the answers don't change much: Every one of them wants their own children to exceed them in their quality of life. It's this very notion that drives the importance of engaging families in the academic lives of their children.

The complicated nature of schooling dictates that educators consider the notion of family engagement as a conduit to improved academic outcomes in the same manner they consider other academic, curricular, and instructional reforms. Promoting the efficacy of families to assist in the learning lives of their children taps into the most influential teacher(s) in a child's life: *their parent(s) and families.*

Every family wants a better life for their children. Engaging families with schools is our best bet to make that happen. Not doing so because there is a chance that a very small percentage of families might not welcome our efforts to engage them doesn't seem prudent.

CASE STUDY: ERNEST B.

Read the case study below. At the conclusion, answer, reflect on, or discuss the questions posed.

Ernest B. was the third of three African American brothers who attended the local high school. His two older brothers dropped out of high school and the oldest brother was serving time in jail for a drug-related crime. Ernest did not know his father and lived with his mother and one brother in a one-room low-income apartment. Ernest's mother held a job, but income was woefully inadequate for the family.

Desperate, Ernest made the poor decision to steal a purse from a woman he saw walking down the street. Ernest was unsuccessful in his larceny attempt, was caught, arrested, and placed in juvenile detention to await a hearing. The following day in school, the principal was alerted to Ernest's situation. Because of the experiences of Ernest's older two brothers, the relationship between Ernest's mother and the principal was very negative. Any attempt to reach out to Ernest's mother usually ended up in a shouting match or worse. Yet Ernest sitting in a jail cell ate away at the principal for most of the day.

Later that day, the principal made a decision to visit Ernest in jail. Upon arrival, the guard opened a gate to allow the principal to enter a group of cells, one of which housed Ernest. Ernest told the guard not to open the cell door because he did not want the principal anywhere near him. Ernest sat on his cot with his elbows on his knees and his head in his hands looking downward toward the floor.

"Ernest, I came here for two reasons today," said the principal. Ernest didn't move or respond. "I'm here because I care about you and I want you to know that regardless of what happens, the sun will rise tomorrow and it will be a new day and a new chance." With those comments, Ernest stood, approached the bars and stared directly into the principal's eyes. His face was filled with rage.

"You care about me? Really? You come all this way to hand me that line of crap? Well, let me show you how much I care about you." With that, Ernest spit on the principal's shirt. Ernest yelled, swore, and became uncontrollably violent in his cell, so much so, the guard came to the cell and was about to open the door and subdue Ernest. At that moment, Ernest fell onto his bed and sobbed. Ernest cried like never before. The principal was quite shocked at the behavior. Ernest begged the principal to help him and the principal vowed that he would.

"What can I do for you right now?" said the principal.

"Please fetch my momma," said Ernest, still sobbing.

At that moment, the principal was confronted with a dilemma. How was he supposed to get Ernest's mother when he knew she hated him and blamed him for the problems her older sons faced and undoubtedly would blame him for Ernest's troubles as well? She was never engaged positively with the school, never attended a conference or event, and never answered any teacher when they attempted to communicate. Teachers had long ago given up on communicating with Ernest's mother.

She defended the actions of her sons and continually blamed the school and, specifically, the principal for the problems that her sons faced. She had called for the principal's firing and accused him of everything from incompetence to racism. Instinctively though, regardless of how difficult a visit, he knew he had to go to the home and talk with Ernest's mother.

The principal called his office to inform his secretary that he was headed over to Ernest B.'s house. His secretary asked him if he needed the police. He assured her he did not. He arrived at the apartment complex and walked up three flights of stairs and stared at the apartment door. After collecting himself, he knocked. The door was fastened with a chain that allowed it to open just a few inches, enough for Ernest's mother to see who was standing there.

"What do you want?" she snapped.

"I came here to talk with you about Ernest," said the principal. After an exchange of unpleasant comments, the door closed, the chain was removed and the door opened. Ernest's mother had already walked away and sat in a chair at the far side of the room.

"So you want to talk about Ernest? Why? Why do you care about my baby boy? He's in jail, right where you want him. Now he ain't gonna be no problem for you no more." Her steely glare made the principal very uncomfortable.

"I understand that you are angry with me, but I have come here because neither one of us alone can help Ernest. We can only do it together. For the sake of your son, can we talk about how to help him?"

"Let me tell you something," started Ernest's mother. "I wouldn't trust you as far as I could throw you. Do you know that when I go to sleep at night, I have a dream? I dream of Ernest graduating from school. And just as he reaches for the diploma, I wake up. I know it's God's way of telling me it ain't ever going to happen. And that is your fault. Now get out of my house before I call the cops and have you arrested for trespassing."

As he walked toward the door, the principal turned and said, "If you change your mind, please come and see me."

"Get out!" the woman yelled as she slammed and chained the door behind the principal.

Two weeks later sitting in his office mired in paperwork, the principal didn't notice a figure standing in his doorway.

"I'm here."

The principal looked up and saw Ernest's mother. He offered her a seat, but she refused. They talked for a few moments about strategies to help Ernest.

"They let him out. Are you going to let him back?" she asked.

"Of course, but only if we figure out how we are going to work together to help Ernest. It would be nice if you came by more often." The principal waited for a response.

"The bus goes right by here so I guess I can do that."

The principal spoke on Ernest's behalf at Ernest's hearing, and he was sentenced to probation. Over the next weeks, months, and years, Ernest's mother, the principal,

(Continued)

(Continued)

and his teachers developed a better relationship, and Ernest managed to attend school, do his work, and for the most part, stay out of significant trouble.

Four years later, Ernest graduated from high school. Four years after that, Ernest graduated from college, the first to do so in his entire family. Ernest invited the principal to his college graduation party held in the basement of the local church. There were few people there to celebrate Ernest's success. Present were one brother, the few distant relatives who could make the trip, and a few church volunteers. Ernest's mother approached the principal.

"What do you want?" said Ernest's mother, exactly as she had several years earlier. The principal became nervous, thinking that the animosity that had dominated their early relationship was still very much real. Ernest's mother turned her stare to a smile, laughed, and grabbed a hand of the principal between both of hers.

"Thank you for saving my baby," she said, with tears forming in her eyes.

"I didn't save him," responded the principal. "We did."

Questions for Reflection

1. How does the story make you feel about what you do?

2. What made the principal visit Ernest in jail?

3. What made the principal visit Ernest's mother?

4. The outcome of this story is a positive one. What key actions played a role in the positive outcome?

5. What belief system did Ernest possess? His mother? The principal? How did their beliefs change over time?

6. What do you think is a key ingredient that made the outcome of this story a positive one?

7. Had the principal never visited Ernest's mother, what do you think the outcome would have been?

4

The Five Simple Principles Explained

DETERMINING A STARTING POINT

Essential to the practice of increasing family engagement is understanding that it truly can be assessed and measured. As is the case with all of the outcomes we desire for our students, it is important to have a starting point to determine "where we are" so goals can be set for "where we want to be."

The following questions are by no means comprehensive in assessing the degree to which your school is successful in engaging every family. They are designed to give you a snapshot, a starting point on your journey to improve the learning outcomes of every student through positive and supportive relationships and engagement with every family.

Directions

For each of the ten questions below, rate your answer on a scale of 1 (strongly DISAGREE) to 4 (strongly AGREE). If you don't know or are unsure of an answer, select the "don't know" category.

Read each question carefully. Think about your answer and select a response that mirrors what you know to be true today. Remember, 1 (strongly disagree), 2 (disagree), 3 (agree), 4 (strongly agree), and 5 (don't know).

	Strongly Disagree			Strongly Agree	Don't Know
Every family feels welcome in our school.	O	O	O	O	O
Our stated core values clearly speak to the importance of family engagement.	O	O	O	O	O
I regularly provide tools and resources to families to support learning at home.	O	O	O	O	O
Our school ensures that families have the opportunity to provide feedback before new policies or procedures are created.	O	O	O	O	O
We have few families that seem apathetic toward our school and their children's education.	O	O	O	O	O
I encourage feedback and dialog from every family of the students I serve.	O	O	O	O	O
We value the participation of community members in our school.	O	O	O	O	O
I can easily communicate with families for whom English is not a first language.	O	O	O	O	O
Our school's shared decision-making model is inclusive of every family.	O	O	O	O	O
We have strong business and civic partnerships that support our school.	O	O	O	O	O

This survey, with directions and scoring, is available for download at www.drsteveconstantino.com

Calculating Your Score

Each response carries a point value:

Strongly disagree	1 point
Disagree	2 points
Agree	3 points
Strongly agree	4 points
Don't know	0 points

Add together the score for each question and total that number. For example, if you answered every question "strongly disagree," you would give yourself 1 point for each answer for a total of 10 points (10 questions, 1 point each). For every "don't know" answer, add 0 (zero). Answers in the "don't know" category carry no points.

Use the scale below to determine where your answers fell on a rubric for successfully engaging every family:

Engaging Every Family Response Interval Scale

10–22: Not Evident

Responses that fall within this range indicate little or no evidence that a process for promoting the ongoing engagement of every family is in place or that the culture of the school embraces family engagement as a pathway to improved student outcomes. A significant effort should be employed to build the capacity of staff to understand and implement practices that engage every family.

23–34: Basic

Responses that fall within this range indicate a basic understanding of the importance of family engagement and some evidence that strategies and ideas have been implemented. There may be evidence of culture change to promote family engagement, but it is at best sporadic. A continued commitment to family engagement as a professional learning strand coupled with measurable goals and objectives as a component of the school improvement plan will increase the likelihood of continuous improvement.

35–44: Emerging

Responses that fall within this range suggest that the school is well along in creating systems and processes that consistently engage every family and the culture is accepting of practice. Many staff members are engaging with families and consider this engagement essential to student success. Determine, through survey or other means of data collection, the degree to which all staff are consistent in the application of family engagement principles and create action plans for continued improvement. Look at student learning data to determine where family engagement practice can support growth.

45–50: Proficient

Responses in this category suggest that the school is highly proficient at engaging every family and has the data to prove it. Everyone agrees that the culture of the school is conducive to engaging every family. All staff believes in the importance of engaging families, and data collected from families supports their perception that the school welcomes their engagement. There is clear, consistent, and compelling evidence that family engagement is a significant portion of the school culture and leads to improved learning outcomes for all students.

Suggestions for This Simple Assessment

There are many ways to use this simple assessment. It is a quick way to determine where you are with regard to engaging every family. Even though it is not meant to be comprehensive, the assessment does provide a snapshot of attitudes, actions, and evidence with regard to family engagement. Here are some ideas for use:

If you are reading this book by yourself, ask your immediate teammates or subject colleagues to take the survey.

If you are using this book for a study, have everyone in the study group take the survey and create a comparison of responses.

Have the leadership team of your school take the survey.

Provide a copy of the survey to every staff member.

After completing the book and implementing some ideas, come back to the survey and take it again. How did things change? If they did not change at all, why do you think that is?

Visit **www.drsteveconstantino.com** for copies of the assessment that you can download as many times as you want!

INTRODUCING THE FIVE SIMPLE PRINCIPLES

The Five Simple Principles are born out of a desire and need to further promote the ideals of engaging every family in the educational lives of their children and bring about systemic and more consistent implementation of school family engagement practices. The principles are meant to help educators build the capacity to formulate necessary partnerships with every family to promote improved student achievement and other desired learning outcomes.

For as many years as there has been research in the field of family engagement, there has existed the frustration that successful engagement practices—those that can be directly connected to student achievement—are at best sporadic. Within school districts, there might be a handful of schools that embrace the concept of family engagement and, within a school, perhaps just a handful of teachers doing the same.

The *Principles* are a systemic process that can be overlaid onto schools or school districts so that measureable and tangible results can be recorded and celebrated.

THE LOGIC MODEL

The term *logic model* has its roots in the field of evaluation. As the term suggests, logic models represent the thinking behind a program and its rationale. A logic model's purpose is to communicate an underlying "theory," assumptions, or hypotheses about why the program will work or about why it is a good solution to an identified problem. Logic models are typically diagrams, flow sheets, or some other type of visual schematic that conveys relationships between contextual factors and programmatic inputs, processes, and outcomes (Parsons & Schmitz, 1999).

Figure 4.1 represents a logic model for *Engage Every Family: Five Simple Principles*. The logic model is designed to place into a hierarchal order the principles by which true family engagement and the ultimate development and nurturing of family efficacy can be implemented and measured. The model supports the notion that there is a process to successful family engagement practice.

Each of the principles (within which additional statements are written to support the main idea) falls into a logical sequence of action. In other words, schools and districts wishing to bring about systemic reform in family engagement should begin at the beginning (Principle 1) and follow the model clockwise around the circle.

The following discussion is intended to share the rationale as to why the model is constructed in the manner it is. Subsequent chapters will expand more specifically on the importance of the principles, their placement within the model, and most importantly, how the ideas of the principles can be implemented and sustained.

Figure 4.1   The Logic Model for *Engage Every Family: Five Simple Principles*

Principle #1: A Culture That Engages Every Family

The model clearly delineates creating a culture and climate for family engagement as the first and most important step in a process to bring about systemic reform in family engagement. If the collective beliefs, values, assumptions, actions, attitudes, and rituals within an organization are not supportive of engaging every family, then there is little hope that the strategies assigned to subsequent standards will have any lasting effect.

More often than not, desired change in an organization that often becomes temporary, sporadic, or fleeting has at its root the idea that the change never permeates and alters the culture of the organization. Therefore, the notion of culture as the leading standard is essential for long-term success and growth.

Principle #2: Communicate Effectively and Build Relationships

When an accepting culture is established and fosters the engagement of every family, it seems logical that the necessary relationships with families be built. Within the framework of relationships and the trust that ensues lies the important notion of communication. Research supports clear and consistent two-way communication as an important pillar in family engagement practice.

Relationships with every family are absolutely essential in the consistent engagement of families from grade level to grade level and school to school. Relationships and trust are rooted in distinct, meaningful, and thoughtful systems of communication that relate a value in reaching out and connecting with every family. Communication, for purposes of this principle, also includes the important concept of welcoming environments in schools.

Principle #3: Empower Every Family

In simple terms, one definition of efficacy is the power of one (or some) to produce an effect. In the Five Simple Principles logic model, the principle of empowerment or efficacy takes family engagement to a new level and begins to allow a school district a tangible and concrete approach to collecting data that marries family engagement to student achievement.

Establishing instructional and curricular processes that are inclusive of families begins to allow families to become immersed in school learning and to enhance and support learning at home. If the culture of the district is not accepting of the idea to engage every family and the communication is poor, thus eroding trusting relationships between families and the school, the results will likely produce little in the way of family efficacy.

Principle #4: Engage Every Family in Decision Making

Improvement plans, strategic plans, comprehensive plans, and the idea of school improvement planning has changed over the years and certainly since the advent of the No Child Left Behind Act of 2001. For many years, schools have sought to include families in decision making at the local school level. Common in many school districts are school board-appointed ad-hoc committees or task forces of families and citizens charged with reviewing issues and making sound recommendations to the board. Inherent in all of this is the concept of engaging every family in school-related decision making. On the surface, this can seem to be a daunting and impossible task.

The arguments set forth in a later chapter identify key reasons why every family needs a voice in certain school decisions, and school leaders must put into place mechanisms that ensure every voice will be heard. Returning to the logic model, after a culture of engagement is established and a foundation of relationships and efficacy has been built, creating mechanisms for family engagement in decision making enhances and ensures that policies, procedures, and practices have at their core a support mechanism for engaging every family.

Principle #5: Engage the Greater Community

Many family engagement models include the involvement and engagement of the greater community as a conduit to improving schools. The key to effective community engagement is to first conceptualize what that engagement should look like with a clear delineation of desired outcomes. There are rich and deep resources in most communities; however, many schools and districts struggle in leveraging those resources.

Without the logic model in place and the sequential building of family engagement, the engagement of the greater community makes little sense. Business, civic, and community leaders who cannot determine a specific role for their engagement simply will not become involved in or immerse themselves in the school or district. Setting the stage with the first four standards is an essential pathway to create a community engagement and support program of efforts.

THE FIVE SIMPLE PRINCIPLES FURTHER DEFINED

The key to the Five Simple Principles is the ability to remember them in the correct order and, to the degree possible, implement and evaluate your efforts and success with the same logic model that is prescribed. *Culture, Relationships, Empowerment, Decision Making, and Community*—five simple ideas to which all educators and families can relate and that all can remember.

As cultural underpinnings of your school, these five principles can bring about lasting and effective change in the ability to engage every family. Of course, there is some danger in trying to oversimplify the principles. That could lead to understanding the concept without the ability to truly drill down to the salient points, thus rendering the principles ineffective.

Below is a description of each of the principles. For each of the principles listed, there are clarifying statements to support the principle presented. Later, each of the principles and their clarifying statements will be discussed in more detail.

Principle #1: A Culture That Engages Every Family

Description. The collective beliefs, attitudes, norms, values, actions, and assumptions of the school organization explicitly embrace and are committed to ensuring the notion of families as a foundational core component to improvement and greater student learning and performance. The culture is reflected in artifacts and organizational practices.

> 1.1 The school has created and sustained a culture that is conducive to family engagement through explicit beliefs, actions, norms, values, and assumptions made about the value of families being engaged with their children's school experiences.

> 1.2 A culture of family engagement exists within the school such that policies, programs, practices, and procedures specifically connect families with student learning to support increased achievement and enhance student learning and performance.

> 1.3 A culture of family engagement exists within the school and community that directly and positively impacts the social and emotional growth of all students.

Principle #2: Communicate Effectively and Build Relationships

Description. There is consistent evidence that effective communication and relationship building creates environments in the schools that are welcoming, respectful, and conducive to family engagement. The school places an emphasis on effective communication with every family and stakeholder within the learning community and seeks to build trusting relationships with every family.

> 2.1 The school creates and maintains a welcoming and respectful environment that is inviting, supportive, and encouraging to every family.

> 2.2 The school employs strategies that extend relationship-building opportunities beyond the school walls so that every family can substantially contribute to the education of their children.

2.3 The school ensures that healthy, two-way communication is consistently maintained. A sense of caring to truly collaborate with every family exists as evidenced by numerous mechanisms to allow families to communicate easily and directly with the school.

Principle #3: Empower Every Family

Description. Families are recognized as essential members of the learning team for each student—their participation is welcomed, valued, and encouraged by the school. The school understands that families are important and influential resources because they know their children best.

3.1 The school makes a conscious effort to educate families to play a proactive role in the school life of their child throughout their school career.

3.2 Families participate in the development of the student's learning plan, help assess progress, and provide support for their child's learning.

3.3 Teachers suggest mentoring possibilities for families and use their local knowledge, personal skills, assets, and networks in ways that support the school's program.

Principle #4: Engage Every Family in Decision Making

Description. The school recognizes the entitlement of families to be consulted and participate in decisions concerning their own children. The school is genuinely inclusive in its approach to decision making. It recognizes that this type of process creates a sense of shared responsibility among families, students, community members, and educators.

4.1 The school creates opportunities for families to lead and participate in school learning, consultative, planning, and social and community events.

4.2 The school ensures that families and students have representation on the school's governing body and relevant decision-making groups.

Principle #5: Engage the Greater Community

Description. The school places a strong focus on building and creating partnerships external to the school. The school recognizes the strengths and talents that exist in the communities that influence student learning and development and seeks to use these to strengthen and support the school, students, and their families.

The principle also recognizes that the school can be a focal point for communities to come together and engage in capacity-building and renewal. The school views itself as an important community asset and has community representatives on the school's governing body. There is a clear recognition from the school that the greater community plays an integral role in the educational success of the school.

5.1   Partnerships are made with individuals and organizations in work and community places to take on mentoring roles within student internship and work placement programs. The partnerships also have a role to play within other activities, such as community-based learning projects, guest speaker programs, job shadows, apprenticeship opportunities, and tutors.

5.2   Partnerships are made with other learning institutions—other schools, technical colleges, universities, and other training providers in order for students to pursue learning opportunities, build their skills, and achieve learning credentials.

5.3   Opportunities evolve from the school for creating and implementing adult learning and community development courses to be run within the school building.

What will follow is a more in-depth discussion of each of the principles and descriptions of best practices, allowing every school to determine their present level of performance and set goals with metrics for improvement.

Descriptions of these principles are available for download at www.drsteveconstantino.com

Principle #1

A Culture That Engages Every Family

> *Alike as schools may be in many ways, each school has an ambiance (or culture) of its own and, further, its ambience may suggest to the careful observer useful approaches to making it better.*
>
> —John Goodlad

THE ILLUSION THAT IS CULTURE

In most organizations, culture is not among the daily thoughts of its members. We don't normally dwell on or think about it. We pass through each day on normal and established routines and barely give notice to how the culture, which is all around us, is shaping everything we do. Nor do we notice our role in defining and shaping the culture within which we work.

One of the great cognitive illusions is titled *L'egs-istential Quandary* created by Roger Shepard and first published in his book *Mind Sights* in 1990. I bet you are familiar with this famous illusion. Take a

> **Principle #1: A Culture That Engages Every Family**
>
> **Description.** The collective beliefs, attitudes, norms, values, actions, and assumptions of the school organization explicitly embrace and are committed to the notion of families as a foundational core component to improvement and greater student learning and performance. The culture is reflected in actions of those in the organization, in the artifacts, and in the organizational practices.
>
> 1.1 The school has created and sustained a culture that is conducive to family engagement through explicit beliefs, actions, norms, values, and assumptions made about the value of families being engaged with their children's school experiences.
>
> 1.2 A culture of family engagement exists within the school such that policies, programs, practices, and procedures specifically connect families with student learning to support increased achievement and enhance student learning and performance.
>
> 1.3 A culture of family engagement exists within the school and community that directly and positively impacts the social and emotional growth of all students.

look by going to this website: http://www.anopticalillusion.com/2012/03/impossible-elephant/. Looking at the picture, ask yourself this question: How many legs does the elephant have? This is even more fun if you try this in a small group of people. Record the number of different answers you get. Depending on how you look at the picture, the number of legs seems to change. The closer you look, the more puzzling it gets! Understanding organizational culture is not dissimilar in its complexity.

Upon a cursory glance, the culture of our organization can seem to be one thing. In the case of engaging families, it is easy to make a quick assumption that we are doing a pretty good job. But when we stop and take a close look and examine the culture carefully, we may very well see something completely different. We see now, things that have always been there, but have gone undetected. We make assumptions about the culture, and often the culture, like an illusionary illustration, can deceive us. Sometimes the culture within which we work deceives us as well.

Every organization, including schools, has a culture of its own. In most cases, the culture has evolved over time. Sadly, in many instances, school culture is not inclusive of every family. For whatever reasons, and there are many varied ones, cultures that embrace the notion of truly engaging every family are not the norm. Without a culture that embraces family engagement, success for every student will undoubtedly remain yet another illusion.

CULTURES AND SUBCULTURES

Inside any school organization, subunits, such as departments, teams, groups, hierarchical levels, and so forth, reflect their own unique cultures. Difficulties in coordinating and integrating processes or organizational activities, for example, are often a result of culture clashes among different subunits.

Interestingly, families are also subunits of schools. They bring their own unique attitudes, beliefs, and culture, and their behavior can be dictated by the behaviors and attitudes of the employees within the school.

Deal and Peterson (1999) provide a simple sentence that speaks volumes about the notion of the importance of sustained positive culture: *"The culture of an enterprise plays the dominant role in exemplary performance"* (p. 1).

Numerous authors, thinkers, and researchers have put their stamp on school culture. In 1932 Willard Waller wrote the following:

> Schools have a culture that is definitely their own. There are, in the school, complex rituals of personal relationships, a set of folkways, mores and irrational sanctions, a moral code based upon them. There are games, which are sublimated wars, teams, and an elaborate set of ceremonies concerning them. There are traditions, and traditionalists waging their world-old battle against innovators. (as cited in Sims and Sims, 2004, p. 141)

Another description of school culture emanates from Boyd (1992), who defines culture as the encompassing attitudes and beliefs of those both inside and outside the school. Also included are the cultural norms of the school and the relationship among persons in the school. Attitude and belief are core issues in the success of any school. Relationships involve actions and interactions of people. These actions are based on attitudes and beliefs, which can also be defined as values.

Culture permeates everything:

- The way people act
- How they dress
- What they talk about or avoid talking about
- Whether they seek out colleagues for help or don't
- How teachers feel about their work, their students, and families of those students

Schein (2010) proposes that culture can be "analyzed at several different levels, with the term *level* meaning the degree to which the cultural phenomenon is visible to the observer" (p. 23). Discussed are three levels of culture, the surface level or artifacts, the intermediary level or espoused beliefs and values, and the final level containing all underlying assumptions within the organization.

There is no question that we are at a crossroads in education. There is the potential to positively reshape and reaffirm the basic tenets of education so that all students benefit from it. Successful schools have at their core a rich and positive school culture. As has been clearly shared, there is

Points to Ponder

Take this opportunity to record your thoughts regarding the three levels of culture in your organization and how the culture relates to engaging every family.

1. What artifacts within your organization speak to the culture in your school and its acceptance of family engagement?
2. What espoused beliefs and values do you think are predominant in your organization with regard to family engagement?
3. What basic underlying assumptions does your organization hold that shape its present culture with regard to family engagement?

no real reform without a permanent shift in culture, and part of that shift must be family engagement.

Research continues to support the notion that creating a demanding culture that includes relational trust and a positive school climate for students and their families is essential for continuous improvement (Fullan, 2001; Bryk & Schneider, 2002; Gonder & Hymes, 1994). Some attempts at improving schools are failing because little attention is being paid to improving the culture of schools. Re-culturing is essential to school change and improvement.

School personnel who can apply a panoramic or holistic view to their schools will better understand the concept of culture and how it applies a context for understanding the complexities and problems that affect schools, especially the delicate relationships that are necessary to move the organization forward. We must hold ourselves accountable for assessing the quality of our own school culture, especially as it relates to family engagement.

CULTURAL CHALLENGES

Schools that do not include the fundamental changes to culture necessary to allow families to fully engage with their children are doomed to implement endless strategies that have shortened life-spans and ultimately produce no long-lasting results.

For as many years as researchers have been writing about family engagement and its importance to overall student achievement and school improvement, schools have been desperately trying to engage every family with less than stellar results. Researchers have offered numerous strategies for schools to implement so that more families, especially those that are traditionally disengaged with their children's education, can become engaged and attached to the school so that their child's learning improves.

While there is no argument that progress has been made with regard to understanding the importance of family engagement and attaining the empirical evidence that it is indeed important, to suggest that real family engagement is ingrained in the culture of every school is an overstatement.

Why then have we had so much trouble with successfully infusing family engagement practices with schools?

The answer lies in one word: culture.

Points to Ponder

Answer these questions from your own perspective, then share thoughts with colleagues.

1. What do I think about family engagement?
2. Will family engagement work at this school? Why or why not?
3. What is my role in promoting family engagement at our school?
4. Am I willing to rearrange time, resources, and energy to work on family engagement to bring about more achievement of my students?

BREAKING THE CYCLE

Most educators quietly acknowledge that over the years numerous ideas have been implemented to help students learn better and achieve more. Every year, school and district leaders stand before the collective body and announce those ideas that will be initiated that year. Many, especially those who have been in education for a long period of time, instinctively know that by year's end most if not all of the initiatives will be gone or at best show little result for the effort and cost.

It is at this juncture that an important question needs to be asked: Why? The answer is simple: Initiatives do not last because the culture of organizations never changes to embrace and sustain the idea. Ideas, objectives, initiatives, and strategies that represent a fundamental antithesis toward the existing culture will always succumb to the existing culture unless significant work is done to augment, expand, and change the culture to embrace the desired change. Courageous leadership is needed to permanently change a culture. Culture can eat change for lunch.

In order to allow family engagement to be the important component to school reform that research has proven it must be, changing the culture of the school to be accepting and inclusive of family engagement is critical.

These simple questions help to get to the core of beliefs about family engagement. More often than not, educators create opinions and perceptions of family engagement based on prior experiences. If the majority of interactions that teachers and other school staff have with families are negative, then it stands to reason that teachers and school staff, over time, will develop negative perceptions of families or at least those that are traditionally disengaged. Worse yet, these experiences can cause teachers and school staff to resign themselves to operating in a culture that does not engage families, because the task seems ominous or has little return value for the effort.

How many times has a principal of a school started the school year by asking all teachers to make five positive phone calls a week? And how many of those phone calls were really made after the first week or two of school? In order to create a culture for families, a thorough understanding that our actions within the organization impact the organization is critical. Then and only then can an organization move forward to create a culture that is truly reflective of valuing the partnership and empowerment of all families.

Think back to a story shared at the beginning of this book—the discussion between an educator and his friend about the move from a public school to a charter school. The simple notion of caring was the root of the parent making a fairly dramatic decision. The actions of the people within the organization could have prevented the move from ever occurring.

If we truly desire families to be engaged with schools and in the academic lives of their children, then we must work to change the culture of schools so that the process of educating children is more humanized. If we are to succeed, we have to be responsive to the individual, regardless of their background of origin.

This change, however, requires that those involved understand and desire the need for the change itself and take ownership in the process. An educational setting that can measure and assess progress with shared goals, shared power, respect for human dignity, and cooperation is well on its way to reshaping their culture forever.

SCHOOL CULTURE DEFINED

Theorists, scholars, researchers, and authors have argued about the meaning of culture for hundreds of years. According to famed anthropologist Clifford Geertz (1973), culture represents a historically transmitted pattern of meaning. Culture is passed on from generation to generation primarily by parents and educational systems of particular societies (Haviland, 1975). This process is often referred to as *enculturation*.

Schein (2010) defines culture as the shared assumptions and ideologies of an organization, with the basic assumption being that everyone is responsible for the future of children. Culture is interchanged with the words climate, ethos, and saga (Deal, 1993). The definition of culture must also include deep patterns of values, beliefs, and traditions that have been formed over the course of the school's history (Deal & Peterson, 1990).

The beliefs of teachers, students and principals transcend the business of creating an efficient learning environment to focus more on the core values necessary to teach students. The distinctive identity of an organization is derived directly from its culture (Schein, 2010).

Considering these ideas, one definition of school culture has at its core the historically transmitted patterns of meaning that include norms, values, beliefs, ceremonies, rituals, traditions, and myths and how well these ideas are understood or engrained in the members of the organization (Stolp & Smith, 1994). Simply put then, culture shapes what people think and how they act and is shaped by the very same. School culture can be summarized as follows:

- School culture does affect the behavior and achievement of elementary and secondary school students
- School culture does not fall from the sky; it is created and thus can be manipulated by people within the school
- School cultures are unique; no two are exactly alike
- School culture becomes the cohesion that bonds the school together
- Culture can be counterproductive and an obstacle to success; culture can also be oppressive for various subgroups
- Lasting change requires a change in the school culture, which is a slow process (Patterson, Purkey, & Parker, 1986)

Wagner (2004/2005) cites three major indicators of improved school culture: collaboration, collegiality, and efficacy, all of which are represented throughout the Five Simple Principles. Central themes include the degree to which people work together and share information, the sense of belonging to an organization, and how members of the organization view themselves within the organization.

These ideas can be easily translated to family engagement: the degree to which schools and families work together, the sense of belonging to the school held by families, and how families view their role within the school organization.

The notion of collaborative school cultures that embrace collegiality and efficacy for all is further supported by understanding that, while all schools are different, most schools continue to exist as isolated places where school staff work alone (Deal & Peterson, 1994). In cultures that foster collaboration, teachers engage with each other. Collaborating with every family is the next logical step.

When determining how to engage every family, collaborative cultures should be inclusive of the important and trusting relationships between school staff and families, which promotes the important ideas of collegiality and efficacy. However, the process to attain this collaborative culture must be real and organic and not contrived.

Focusing on engaging every family is much more prevalent at the school level than it is at the district level. In larger districts, it is quite common for some schools to embrace family engagement and others not. In many school districts, there tends to be more attention to families at the primary level and less at the secondary level. All of these situations detract from creating cultures that support the engagement of every family.

SCHOOL DISTRICT INCONSISTENCY WITH FAMILIES

As an example, let's take the fictitious Marshall family. The Marshalls are a fairly engaged family. They have one child in school, Joseph. Joseph's teacher, Mrs. Knight, is a teacher who supports the notion of engaging every family. She makes building relationships with families a priority.

The Marshalls feel comfortable with Mrs. Knight and, as a result, Joseph is doing quite well. Mrs. Knight is communicative, creates opportunities for parents to engage with their children's schoolwork, helps parents preview upcoming work, and makes numerous telephone calls and home visits to all families. The Marshalls and Joseph have a wonderful year in Mrs. Knight's class.

The following year, Joseph is assigned to Mr. Bradford. Mr. Bradford is an excellent teacher but does not subscribe to the engage every family mentality. The Marshalls do not have the access or relationship with Mr. Bradford. Mr. Bradford does not make phone calls unless a problem occurs in school and sends home only work that has been completed with no previewing of upcoming work. He does not make home visits.

Even though Mr. Bradford is a fine teacher, the Marshalls do not believe he is as effective as Mrs. Knight. The Marshalls become increasingly frustrated, and the relationship between the Marshalls and Mr. Bradford grows tense, because the Marshalls expected to have the same experience they had with Mrs. Knight.

While this story is fictitious and designed to illustrate a point, the lack of *systemic* attention to family engagement effectively "undoes" any work by individual schools or teachers who are promoting the ideas of engaging every family. The answer to this inconsistent pattern is for the school district to adopt policies, procedures, and practices that support the notion of engaging every family to enhance student achievement.

START WITH POLICY

Today, family engagement is an integral part of school reform and improved student achievement. For many years, family engagement scored a relatively low priority among the nation's school districts. As of late, that is all changing (Mapp & Kuttner, 2013). Meaningful and actionable policy at the school district level can bring about the levels of family engagement that have often eluded and frustrated schools and districts, especially when trying to engage all types of families. Educators report initiatives in family engagement as among their most challenging work (Markow, Macia, & Lee, 2013).

It is imperative that thoughtful, meaningful, and engaging family engagement policy is created in all school districts. Unlike most policies, family engagement policy is created in what can be termed as a dual-capacity manner, meaning the school district recognizes the importance of a shared responsibility with families and enacts policies that are both developed and implemented by the school district and the families that they serve (Mapp & Kutner, 2013).

Mapp and Kutner (2013) proposed that in order to effectively develop policy in a shared manner, challenges must be overcome. First, educators need training and capacity building in the area of family engagement. Families who are traditionally disengaged with schools are a focus of the capacity building, such that policy development truly represents the voices of the school district and their families.

School districts wishing to imbed a true culture of family engagement must start with a review of their existing policies, rules, and regulations to determine "where they are" and must then determine, with the help of all constituents, "where they wish to be." This process is illustrated by the example below:

Policy Component	Desired State
Engaging every family in policy development	Family engagement policy ensures that families for whom the policies are written have an essential voice in the design of the policy. In order to do so, the school district makes the effort to garner the opinions and wisdom of all families, especially those who may be either traditionally disengaged from learning or underrepresented in school-level decision making. Through actions such as focus groups and planning teams, families and educators work side by side to discuss and create meaningful policy.
Ensuring assistance with federal and state standards in family engagement	There is an increasing focus nationally on the importance of engaging families in the educational lives of their children. School districts wishing to develop comprehensive policy must create pathways for school personnel and families to clearly understand the expectations of federal and state policy in family engagement. To do so means the policy must demand effective family engagement practices, measureable outcomes as a result of family engagement, and accountability on the part of the district for ensuring unilateral implementation of policy that includes the necessary resources.
Creating goals to engage every family	*What gets measured gets done.* The school district is responsible for creating specific goals related to family engagement and, with those goals, there is an expectation of measurement of success or effectiveness. Items like the extent and type of family engagement expected should be spelled out in policy. At the core of the policy goals are those family engagement best practices that are directly related to improved student achievement.

(Continued)

(Continued)

Policy Component	Desired State
Engaging every family as the core of continuous improvement	The degree to which families are engaged should be assessed annually, and district policy should specify the annual assessment. Specific goals created (perhaps in the district strategic plan or school-level improvement plans) should be assessed by both school personnel and families. The relationship of the academic achievement of students and the involvement of their families is an integral part of the assessment. A model of continuous improvement should be established to collect the data and make midcourse adjustments to policies and practice.
Engaging every family in every school	It is common for procedures and requirements in family engagement to be relegated to Title I schools only, given family engagement's role in the federal grant program. Meaningful policy development has at its core an expectation for all schools within the district to develop and implement measurable goals and practices in family engagement. District policy goals can be embedded in each school plan and become part of the overall evaluation of school performance.
Assisting every family	School district family engagement policy asserts that meaningful and relevant partnerships that provide support and assistance for every family are sustained within every school. Policy supports the idea that families have a true sense and understanding of state academic standards and requirements and any local achievement standards that have been implemented. Other items such as a program of study, course and curricular material, and other information that teaches and builds capacity of families to understand and be meaningfully involved in their child's academic experiences is also included. Lastly, the district policy ensures that the information is understandable and easily accessible by every family (modes of delivery, use of technology, language, etc.). Where possible, policies can include the creation of family resource centers in the district or community, which can help disseminate and support family understanding of academic programs and requirements.
Engaging every family in parenting skills	School district policy development should include the recognition that parenting skills are important to successful family engagement and student achievement in school and include specific language to support this important aspect. The policy should support professional development of all staff to build the capacity to create and sustain effective parenting practices for every family. Further, the policy should include support for funding to help improve parenting in the district. The policy should also support a parent-training component as well.
Every family has a voice	Meaningful and effective school district family engagement policy directs that families have specific roles in the governance of all schools. The policy should contain specific language about family engagement in governance and decision making and describe a clear process for monitoring. The policy should make a conscious effort to be inclusive of every family and support the capacity building of schools to do the same.

Policy Component	Desired State
District policy supports professional development to build the capacity for family engagement	School district policy directs the ongoing and meaningful professional development and capacity building of staff as a critical foundation to engaging every family. The policy should clearly articulate the district's expectation that schools include family engagement professional development for all professional and support staff and include families in the program. Specific professional development programs for families are also included as an important policy component.
Funding the engagement of every family	School district family engagement policy supports and specifies district and site budget lines to the effective development, implementation, and measurement of district and school-based family engagement programs. All aspects of the district and building budget development process have embedded into them family engagement sections to ensure an ongoing commitment and continuous improvement in engaging every family.

Source: Adapted with permission from NCPIE. Available for download at www.drsteveconstantino.com

Use the following chart to determine where your school or district is with policy development and what steps you might take to create a desired state as listed above.

Policy Component	Desired State	Present State	Actions Needed
Engaging every family in policy development	Family engagement policy ensures that families for whom the policies are written have an essential voice in the design of the policy. In order to do so, the school district makes the effort to garner the opinions and wisdom of all families, especially those who may be either traditionally disengaged from learning or underrepresented in school-level decision making. Through actions such as focus groups and planning teams, families and educators work side by side to discuss and create meaningful policy.		

(Continued)

(Continued)

Policy Component	Desired State	Present State	Actions Needed
Ensuring assistance with federal and state standards in family engagement	There is an increasing focus nationally on the importance of engaging families in the educational lives of their children. School districts wishing to develop comprehensive policy must create pathways for school personnel and families to clearly understand the expectations of federal and state policy in family engagement. To do so means the policy must demand effective family engagement practices, measureable outcomes as a result of family engagement, and accountability on the part of the district for ensuring unilateral implementation of policy that includes the necessary resources.		
Creating goals to engage every family	*What gets measured gets done.* The school district is responsible for creating specific goals related to family engagement and, with those goals, there is an expectation of measurement of success or effectiveness. Items like the extent and type of family engagement expected should be spelled out in policy. At the core of the policy goals are those family engagement best practices that are directly related to improved student achievement.		

Policy Component	Desired State	Present State	Actions Needed
Engaging every family as the core of continuous improvement	The degree to which families are engaged should be assessed annually, and district policy should specify the annual assessment. Specific goals created (perhaps in the district strategic plan or school-level improvement plans) should be assessed by both school personnel and families. The relationship of the academic achievement of students and the involvement of their families is an integral part of the assessment. A model of continuous improvement should be established to collect the data and make midcourse adjustments to policies and practice.		
Engaging every family in every school	It is common for procedures and requirements in family engagement to be relegated to Title I schools only, given family engagement's role in the federal grant program. Meaningful policy development has at its core an expectation for all schools within the district to develop and implement measurable goals and practices in family engagement. District policy goals can be embedded in each school plan and become part of the overall evaluation of school performance.		

(Continued)

(Continued)

Policy Component	Desired State	Present State	Actions Needed
Assisting every family	School district family engagement policy asserts that meaningful and relevant partnerships that provide support and assistance for every family are sustained within every school. Policy supports the idea that families have a true sense and understanding of state academic standards and requirements and any local achievement standards that have been implemented. Other items such as a program of study, course and curricular material, and other information that teaches and builds capacity of families to understand and be meaningfully involved in their child's academic experiences is also included. Lastly, the district policy ensures that the information is understandable and easily accessible by every family (modes of delivery, use of technology, language, etc.). Where possible, policies can include the creation of family resource centers in the district or community that can help disseminate and support family understanding of academic programs and requirements.		

Policy Component	Desired State	Present State	Actions Needed
Engaging every family in parenting skills	School district policy development should include the recognition that parenting skills are important to successful family engagement and student achievement in school and include specific language to support this important aspect. The policy should support professional development of all staff to build the capacity to create and sustain effective parenting practices for every family. Further, the policy should include support for funding to help support improved parenting in the district. The policy should also support a parent-training component as well.		
Every family has a voice	Meaningful and effective school district family engagement policy directs that families have specific roles in the governance of all schools. The policy should contain specific language about family engagement in governance and decision making and describe a clear process for monitoring. The policy should make a conscious effort to be inclusive of every family and support the capacity building of schools to do the same.		

(Continued)

(Continued)

Policy Component	Desired State	Present State	Actions Needed
District policy supports professional development to build the capacity for family engagement	School district policy directs the ongoing and meaningful professional development and capacity building of staff as a critical foundation to engaging every family. The policy should clearly articulate the district's expectation that schools include family engagement professional development for all professional and support staff and include families in the program. Specific professional development programs for families are also included as an important policy component.		
Funding the engagement of every family	School district family engagement policy supports and specifies district and site budget lines to the effective development, implementation, and measurement of district and school-based family engagement programs. All aspects of the district and building budget development process have embedded into them family engagement sections to ensure an ongoing commitment and continuous improvement in engaging every family.		

Source: Adapted with permission from NCPIE. Available for download at www.drsteveconstantino.com

DEVELOPING STRATEGIC PLAN GOALS: WHAT GETS MEASURED GETS DONE

From policies and rules come the goals and objectives that create actionable and measurable improvements in family engagement. Remember the old adage, "what gets measured gets done." Without measurement, it is unlikely that any effort in family engagement will produce outcomes that are sustainable or, more importantly, create a permanent change in the culture of the district or its schools. (We will be putting this to work in Chapter 10.)

It can be a bit daunting to create goals and objectives at the district level that do not micromanage but keep the focus on the district and its improvement. For example, here is an actual goal statement lifted from a district strategic plan:

The numbers of parents involved in the PTA will increase.

The district that created this goal had wonderful intentions. They knew that getting parents engaged in the PTA would bring more parents to school and thus more parents engaged with the school and learning. However, counting up the number of people who sign up for the PTA may or may not bring about increased academic achievement of all students.

Perhaps a better goal statement might be the following:

To assist with the increase in academic achievement of all students, every school will design and promote opportunities for home/ school interaction focused on student learning that will result in a 5% increase in family participation.

The second statement allows for every school to create their own goals based on their data, community, and specific needs. If a school already has 98% of the families joining the PTA, then the district goal statement does not provide a great deal of direction for that particular school. However, the second statement allows every school to assess where they are and create goals that are meaningful and relevant to their school.

Perhaps more family engagement in content-specific workshops might be in order, or an increase in the numbers of families attending and participating in student conferences is an appropriate goal. Regardless of what the district decides, their mission is to remain *strategic* and avoid becoming *tactical*.

Activity: School Culture Grids: Present and Desired Perceptions of Culture

Now that you have read and reflected on the importance of culture in your school or district, it's time to determine where you are and where you want to be. The two charts that appear below will move you toward your desired state by understanding those areas of your culture in need of attention.

Take as much time as necessary for you, your team, or your collective organization to analyze and answer the organizational statement. Hold the statement against the present practices and systems in your school or district. In each case, an example is given to stimulate your thinking. The answers you give, however, are yours and reflect your thinking and the thinking of those with whom you work. Look for areas of agreement and disagreement and come to consensus on how changes in your school culture can help engage every family.

(Continued)

(Continued)

Present Perceptions of Culture

Fill in the grids based on the present state of your organization. Be honest and objective in your answers. Discuss areas of disagreement and come to consensus. Ask families their perceptions as well.

Organizational Statement	Beliefs	Artifact Support	Underlying Values	Notes, Thoughts, Ideas
EXAMPLE: The ability for all children to learn at high levels	There may or may not be general agreement, but we should believe that all children can learn.	Safe and orderly environment, improved test scores, student dress code, displays of student work throughout building	Decision to create new sections for ALL students, yearly review of improvement plan	The achievement gap between regular students and students in special education still exists.
How individuals are valued within your school (adults and children)				
How families are valued within your school				
The ability for all children to learn at high levels				
The manner of decision making (present)				
Diversity				
The responsibility to teach children				
The manner of governance (present)				
The effectiveness of organizational communication				

Organizational Statement	Beliefs	Artifact Support	Underlying Values	Notes, Thoughts, Ideas
The degree to which the organization promotes continuous improvement				

School Culture: Desired School Culture

Now that you have finished determining the present state of the culture of your organization, the next step is to determine where you would *like to be* as an organization. The statements and categories are the same, except this time, you are working toward a *desired state* in each of the areas.

Organizational Statement	Desired Belief Structure	Desired Artifact Support	Desired Underlying Values	Notes, Thoughts, Ideas
EXAMPLE: The ability for all children to learn at high levels	All staff and families will support the explicit notion that all children can learn at high levels, with proper support, relationships, and encouragement.	Redeployment of classes and sizes; large enrollments in advanced offerings, meet grade level objectives for all	All students, not just special education students, should have individual needs plans developed jointly with students, staff, and families. All students who are at risk should receive additional support and encouragement.	
How individuals are valued within your school (adults and children)				
How families are valued within your school				

(Continued)

(Continued)

Organizational Statement	Desired Belief Structure	Desired Artifact Support	Desired Underlying Values	Notes, Thoughts, Ideas
The ability for all children to learn at high levels				
The manner of decision making (present)				
Diversity				
The responsibility to teach children				
The manner of governance (present)				
The effectiveness of organizational communication				
The degree to which the organization promotes continuous improvement				

Each of the desired areas of culture can then become goal statements under which objectives and specific strategies can be created to ensure progress toward the goal.

Source: Used with permission of Dr. Joni Samples, Family Friendly Schools. Charts are available for download at www.drsteveconstantino.com

CULTURE CASE STUDY: THE SCIENCE PROJECT[1]

The case study below is designed to promote conversation and dialog about the ideas presented in this chapter. At the conclusion of the case study, several questions for discussion are listed.

Mary teaches middle school science. She has assigned her students the long-term project of picking one of the planets in the solar system and preparing a display and report to be shared with the class and exhibited at the school "open house." Mary spends considerable time each year on this project. The displays are always well received and the principal always comments about how the project puts the school in a very positive light with the community. The students use their library and writing skills, research skills, and presentation skills, and they coordinate their creativity and ability to conceptualize and apply their knowledge. By all accounts, it is an excellent project.

Some parents have contacted Mary to ask questions about specific aspects of the assignment, trying to determine what Mary's expectation is with regard to the display portion of the project. Mary has become quite used to parent calls and skillfully answers each question to the satisfaction of parents. One parent, Mrs. Smith, explains to Mary that she is on a fixed income and cannot afford the art materials necessary for her child to fully participate in the project. She fears not only a bad grade but that her child will be embarrassed at the open house if the display is not up to the standards of the displays of other students. Mary tries to assure Mrs. Smith that whatever her child produces will be acceptable, provided that the guidelines of the assignment are followed.

Mary indicates that the project should be driven by the child, not the parent, and that Mrs. Smith should support her child but not worry about the amount of money spent or the "glitz factor" of the final project. Presentation boards and construction paper will be supplied by the school.

Even though the conversation was pleasant, Mary sensed that Mrs. Smith was not completely comfortable with her responses. Mary mentioned to the principal that there is a chance he might hear from Mrs. Smith. She explained the situation to the principal and the principal thanked her for the "heads up." No further conversation took place.

Mrs. Smith was not convinced that this assignment was fair and takes her concern to the principal. The principal listens to Mrs. Smith and assures her that there will be no repercussion if significant money is not spent nor will there be preferential treatment for different displays of creativity within the project. Feeling that she can do nothing more, she leaves the principal's office calm but frustrated.

Mrs. Smith supports and works with her child for several weeks to help create the best display and report possible. The Smith family does not have a home computer or printer. The family car is taken to work by Mr. Smith, who works the three to eleven in the evening shift at the local warehouse; therefore driving to the library is not possible. Mrs. Smith asked if her daughter could use a computer at school and was told yes, but the school could not allow the students to print the reports, since it had a limited paper and ink budget for the computers. Mrs. Smith, remembering that writing was an important aspect of the assignment, encouraged her child to use her best penmanship and write the assignment by hand on notebook paper. Mrs. Smith directed her daughter to write neatly and legibly or the process would begin again.

Mrs. Smith's child turned in a project on time. Her child received a grade of "85" on the project.

When Mrs. Smith came to the open house, she quickly saw that many of the projects were indeed elaborate . . . a paper-mache model of Mars, complete with canyons and craters, color photographs and a report done on a computer and printed in color. There were planets spinning on battery-powered spindles representing an axis and one that was able to form the gaseous clouds of the planet's atmosphere, because of a parent's expertise in atmospheric engineering.

Mrs. Smith noticed that her child's project was not among the others. When she asked Mary, Mary indicated that there was not enough room in the hallway for all of the projects and that some were displayed in the classroom. Upon entering the classroom, Mrs. Smith noticed that the three projects in the classroom, including her child's project, had no special effects and the reports were handwritten. While they met the spirit of the assignment, they were obviously not as elaborate as the others on public display in the hallway.

Confirming her worst fears, Mrs. Smith was angry at the situation and made no effort to conceal her emotions toward Mary and the principal. Her child, embarrassed by the entire situation, left the school building and waited outside until Mrs. Smith was finished yelling at the teacher and the principal. The principal asked Mrs. Smith and Mary to step into his office. He told Mrs. Smith that her child received a "good grade" and that her behavior was inappropriate toward Mary and him.

Mary was in tears, and Mrs. Smith was close to tears. The principal told Mrs. Smith that there was nothing wrong with the display configuration and that Mary was an excellent teacher who had prepared these assignments successfully for many years. He believed the entire incident should not have happened and told Mrs. Smith that all she had accomplished was to undermine the relationship between herself and Mary and embarrass her child. Mrs. Smith was unable to express her feelings of inadequacy about the incident, the project, and the fact that what happened was exactly what she feared, given similar situations in past years.

Feeling outnumbered and outmatched, Mrs. Smith left the principal's office, found her child, and went home. Her child was absent from school the next day.

Questions for Reflection

1. Given what you have learned about the culture, how would you characterize the culture of this school? (Consider beliefs, values, assumptions, actions, and attitudes of all.)

2. Based on your opinions and answers with regard to the above question, what specific information in the story led you to the conclusions you made? Be specific.

3. The story depicts a school project that, for at least one family, went horribly wrong. What steps could have been taken to prevent what happened in the story?

4. What specific changes in culture do you see that are necessary to provide a different outcome to this situation?

5. If you had to surmise the attitudes of the principal and teacher toward family engagement, what would you think their attitudes were?

6. Do you think the principal supports family engagement in the school?

7. What was the purpose of the project? Why did it exist?

8. Given what you have read and discussed, could this situation happen in your school? Why or why not?

An Added Tip for Changing School Culture

The need to examine school culture as a vehicle for school improvement is a concept that school personnel should embrace with or without family engagement strategies as a focus. The depth of understanding about how to examine and shape school culture goes far beyond what can be printed here.

Terrance Deal and Kent Peterson are two researchers, authors, and experts in the field of organizational culture. It is highly recommended that you delve further into the ideas of organizational culture as an important conduit to ultimate success in your school. Below are two books that are not only resources and inspirations for this chapter but also excellent books to use when looking to make changes in culture.

Deal, T. E., & Peterson, K. D. (1999). *Shaping school culture: The heart of leadership*. New Jersey: John Wiley and Sons.
Peterson, K. D. & Deal, T. E. (2009). *The shaping school culture field book (2nd. ed.)*. New Jersey: John Wiley and Sons.

CREATING A CULTURE TO ENGAGE EVERY FAMILY

Each of the Five Simple Principles have clarifying statements designed to further assist schools with implementation. Subsequent to each one of the statements is a description of best practice with regard to the ideas in the statements. Subsequent to that description are a number of ideas and suggestions on how to go about creating the environment as described.

PRINCIPLE #1: A CULTURE THAT ENGAGES EVERY FAMILY

Description. The collective beliefs, attitudes, norms, values, actions, and assumptions of the school organization explicitly embrace and are committed to ensuring the notion of families as a foundational core component to improvement and greater student learning and performance. The culture is reflected in the actions of those within the organization, in the artifacts, and in the organizational practices.

Where We Are

Based on the description, discuss and record where you think your school is today as it relates to the principle description.

1.1 The school has created and sustained a culture that is conducive to family engagement through explicit beliefs, actions, norms, values and assumptions made about the value of families being engaged with their children's school experiences.

Best Practice Description

The culture at the school consistently provides support for and embraces the notion of engaging every parent and family member rather than settling for those families that are already engaged or those families that are traditionally easier to engage. School leadership has set high standards for the engagement of every family and in tandem with staff, lives by culture statements that reflect the organization's beliefs about the benefits of engaging every family.

Measureable objectives with regard to family engagement are clear. The beliefs of all teaching and support staff sustain the notion that families should be engaged and empowered to have an active role in the education of their children as is evidenced by their consistent actions, attitudes and assumptions.

The norms and values of the organization support the principle of family engagement as an effective and necessary component to overall school improvement, and there is tangible and credible evidence of every family being engaged with all aspects of their children's learning and the operation of the school. Every family feels a strong sense of belonging to the school.

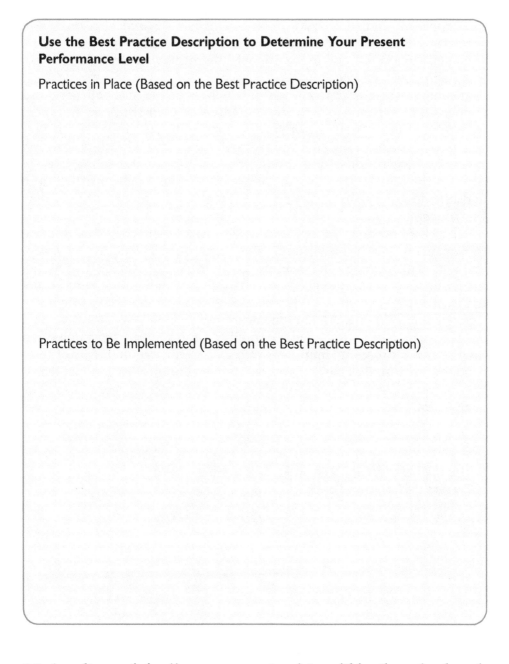

Use the Best Practice Description to Determine Your Present Performance Level

Practices in Place (Based on the Best Practice Description)

Practices to Be Implemented (Based on the Best Practice Description)

1.2 A culture of family engagement exists within the school such that policies, programs, practices, and procedures specifically connect families with student learning to support increased achievement and enhance student learning and performance.

Best Practice Description

There is consistent, tangible, credible, and measurable evidence that the school culture believes in and values the engagement of every family in support of student learning. The school has devised structures and supports to improve student learning and performance outcomes for all students, especially those in traditional subgroups that struggle to attain acceptable achievement.

School staff embraces a culture in which families are encouraged and supported to be partners in the learning lives of their children, and there is consistent and tangible evidence of such with policies and practice. School staff believes in and embraces the idea of a seamless learning process between school and home. The culture of the school clearly denotes families as the first and most influential teachers of children and has designed or redesigned its systems and processes to support this concept.

Teachers and other school staff have formative mechanisms in place to help every family understand what their child is learning in school and how that learning can be supported in the home. Rather than reducing family engagement to event attendance, the school has embraced the notion that engagement with learning outside of the school has the most significant impact on student outcomes.

The school provides ongoing training and support for families to understand and become immersed in the academic requirements of their children, because they believe and value the concept. Professional learning for teachers consistently contains a family engagement strand or component.

Use the Best Practice Description to Determine Your Present Performance Level

Practices in Place (Based on the Best Practice Description)

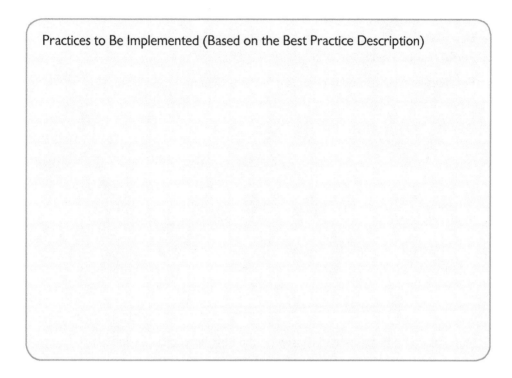

Practices to Be Implemented (Based on the Best Practice Description)

1.3 A culture of family engagement exists within the school and community that directly and positively impacts the social and emotional growth of all students.

Best Practices Description

The culture of the school includes families, community agencies, and non-education partners in the relational growth and development as well as the sense of belonging for all students in school and within the community. With the help of identified resources in the community, clear and consistent support and practices nurture positive and productive relationships between school staff and every family so that all students are cared for and are learning in the appropriate environments.

The culture of school, family, and community relationships has at its core a unified support of the development of the whole child. The climate and practices of the school continually reinforce the growth of families as teachers and supporters of education. The school provides opportunities for parents to develop their skills as parents so that the emotional and social growth of children can extend from school to home.

The school has made a significant commitment to professional learning for all staff that helps all teachers understand the social and emotional growth of children and how family and community relationships enhance the efforts to help all children learn.

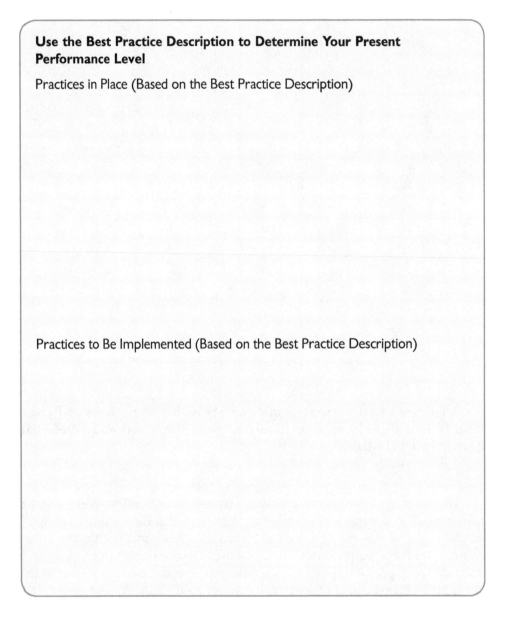

Use the Best Practice Description to Determine Your Present Performance Level

Practices in Place (Based on the Best Practice Description)

Practices to Be Implemented (Based on the Best Practice Description)

NOTE

1. Case study used with permission of Dr. Joni Samples, Family Friendly Schools.

6

Principle #2

Communicate Effectively and Build Relationships

They expect me to go to school so they can tell me my kid is stupid or crazy. They've been telling me that for three years, so why should I go and hear it again? They don't do anything. They just tell me my kid is bad.

—A Father (from Finders and Lewis, 1994)

Let's start out with some easy ideas that promote Principle #2![1]

- Staff training: importance of family involvement (This book is a great start!)
- Community outreach meetings
- Train present parent/family leaders. Include them in school-based trainings.
- Family of the month
- Family hall of fame
- Family week
- Celebrate the community

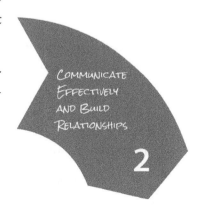

COMMUNICATE EFFECTIVELY AND BUILD RELATIONSHIPS

2

> **Principle #2: Communicate Effectively and Build Relationships**
>
> **Description.** There is consistent evidence that effective communication and relationship building creates environments in the schools that are welcoming, respectful, and conducive to family engagement. The school places an emphasis on effective communication with every family and stakeholder within the learning community and seeks to build trusting relationships with every family.
>
> 2.1 The school creates and maintains a welcoming and respectful environment that is inviting, supportive, and encouraging to every family.
>
> 2.2 The school employs strategies that extend relationship-building opportunities beyond the school walls so that every family can substantially contribute to the education of their children.
>
> 2.3 The school ensures healthy, two-way communication is consistently maintained. A sense of caring to truly collaborate with every family exists as evidenced by numerous mechanisms to allow families to communicate easily and directly with the school.

- Community asset mapping
- Family center
- Family parking
- Welcome signs
- Marquee/foyer
- E-mail
- Website
- Answering machine
- Voicemail
- Call-out device
- Social media uses (Twitter, Facebook, blogs, Wikis, etc.)
- Parents as cultural translators
- Professional development for promoting parent leadership: capacity building
- Parents as interpretive vehicles: concepts into everyday language (Parents and teachers both pick up each other's vocabulary.)

Within *Principle #2, Communicate Effectively and Build Relationships,* there are three core ideas that are essential in developing the principles:

1. Building effective relationships and thus trust with every family

2. Communicating effectively with every family

3. Creating welcoming environments in schools to promote active family engagement

A significant amount of strategies and practice focus on the welcoming environment of a school and/or the need to effectively communicate with families and ensure that the communication is two-way. Principle #2 takes those concepts a step further, suggesting that both of these ideas flourish with better and more trusting relationships with families. For that reason, these three ideas form the basis for the principle. To have a meaningful conversation about two-way communication, technology and social media environments must be considered in the area of relationships and communication.

Activity: What Role Do Communication and Relationships Play in the Success of Your Students?

This short activity is designed to get you thinking about communication and relationships with families and their effects on student learning. Follow the instructions below.

In the first column of boxes below list the top five highest performing students that you presently teach or, if you are not presently teaching, the top five highest performing students you have taught at some point in your career. Next to each student's name and in the second set of boxes to the right of the student's name, think about your relationship and communication with their family. Did the family respond to requests for information? Did they call you? Did you call them? Did they attend conferences and school activities? Did you communicate regularly or as needed? Did you feel positive about the relationships you had with the families of these students that you listed? Would you consider them engaged? These are just a few questions to get you thinking. Jot down any notes or ideas that attaches the student you have listed to the communication and relationship you have/had with their families.

Names of Five Highest Performing Students	Notes on Communication/Relationships With Families of Those Students
1.	
2.	

(Continued)

(Continued)

Names of Five Highest Performing Students	Notes on Communication/Relationships With Families of Those Students
3.	
4.	
5.	

On the next chart, start by listing the top five *lowest performing students* you teach or have taught. Next to each one of those names, use the same process that you used above to determine the communication and relationships you had with the families of this set of students.

Names of the Five Lowest Performing Students	Notes on Communication and Relationships With the Families of Those Students
1.	

2.	
3.	
4.	
5.	

Now that you have completed both charts, compare the notes and ideas you have on the communication and relationships with families. Here are a couple of discussion questions to help you reflect:

1. What similarities and differences are there between the interactions with each set of families?

2. If there are differences, why do you think those differences exist/existed?

3. Do you think there is a correlation between the learning outcomes of each set of students and the communication and relationships you had with each of their families?

(Continued)

> (Continued)
>
> The key to engaging every family is to believe that every family cares about their children and strongly desires that their children exceed them in their quality of life. An understanding of the disengaged is essential to effectively create systems and processes for effectively and efficiently engaging every family. In Chapter 3, we learned about disengagement and how it occurs. Below are more specific ideas and information about family disengagement with school.

Charts are available for download at www.drsteveconstantino.com

IT'S THE LITTLE THINGS

From time to time I have the good fortune to stay in a very posh, upscale hotel. The services these hotels provide are simply over the top. These high-end hotels are focused on one thing: your comfort while there as a guest and the hope you will return soon.

When I open the closet door in my room I sometimes see elegant bathrobes hanging on fancy padded hangers. I always notice a little tag hanging from the robe and hanger and it usually says something like this: *"We are pleased to provide this robe for your use while a guest in our hotel. If you would like to purchase the robe they are available in our gift shop."*

What does that sentence mean?

Exactly. Don't steal the robe! But the message is sent in a very subtle and classy way. Now, let's think about the messages we send to those who visit our schools.

Warning! Trespassers will be prosecuted.

No Skateboarding; No Running; No Motorcycles

All Visitors Must Report to the Main Office

This Parking Lot for Faculty/Staff Only

Your Presence Is Being Recorded

Not so subtle. When we think about the welcoming environment of our schools, we must think about the messages that our visitors receive the minute they enter our property and then our schools. Make sure the words "welcome," "please" and "thank you" are visible:

Welcome to our school! We are glad you are here! Please sign in at our main office. This way (arrow or directions).

Thank you for being here today. We appreciate it. Come back soon! (Sign over the door as people exit.)

While we may think these small gestures are not worth our trouble, we must consider why, then, businesses and retailers all over the globe go out of their way to welcome us and to ensure our experience is a positive one.

And while we are on the subject, is there a difference between a visitor and a guest? Disney seems to think so. Guests are those that have an open invitation and for whose arrival and visit we plan for to ensure a positive experience. A visitor is someone we do not invite or for which we do not plan, with the hope they won't stay long.

CASE STUDY: I KNOW WHAT THEY THINK OF ME

The following short case study is designed to act as a catalyst for discussion regarding relationships with parents. At the conclusion of the case study are questions for discussion.

An urban school district wished to analyze their present commitment to family engagement and then set about trying to improve. The vast majority of families served were disadvantaged economically and represented a myriad of cultures and ethnicities. The teachers were embracing the new commitment to family engagement but, understandably, were skeptical of the outcomes and frustrated with yet another "new initiative."

A group of elementary teachers at one of the schools located in a relatively impoverished neighborhood were in a reporting meeting regarding their initial efforts to engage families. They had gone through the first training modules and were reporting out on their experiences thus far. These teachers were frustrated, indicating they had "tried everything" to engage families and that their success rate was minimal. At one point, a frustrated teacher exclaimed, "We did everything that was suggested. We made home visits, we sent personal invitations, we made the work we were doing relevant to the parents and families, we had food, we had childcare and tutoring, and we even arranged for transportation. After all of that, three parents participated in our workshop. We can't do any more."

The session the teachers were having was with a coach/consultant. The consultant said, "Well then, it looks like we are going to have to figure out why this isn't working. We need to find out why parents and families are not responding to your efforts."

"How will we do that?" the teachers asked.

"We—you and I—are going to go ask them."

Three teachers and the consultant made their way to the home of a parent that did not attend the event as planned. The home was located in a housing project within walking distance of the school. The group arrived at the apartment door and the teachers looked nervously at the consultant.

"Now what?" they asked rather nervously.

(Continued)

(Continued)

"How about we knock on the door?" the consultant answered.

A woman, dressed in a housecoat with curlers in her hair, came to the door and opened it as far as the door chain would allow. When she saw the teachers, she opened the door and invited the group in, looking rather cautiously at the consultant. It was noted the apartment was barely inhabitable, with a broken window, a space heater, and a family of five living in what amounted to two rooms. After a bit of small talk, the consultant took the lead, explaining to the parent why the group had visited her. She was asked if the teachers had told her about the event, they did. She was asked if she knew how the event would eventually help her child, she did. Asked if she had received personal invitations and reminders, she indicated she had. She also knew there was childcare, knew there was food, and knew there was transportation if she needed it. She also freely admitted that she told the teachers she would attend.

"But you didn't attend?" the consultant asked.

"That's right," said the parent.

"May I ask why?"

"Because I know what they all think of me over there."

Questions for Discussion

1. What do you think is lacking in the relationship between the parent and the teachers in the story?

2. What perceived value of building a relationship do the teachers hold? How about the parent? Do you think the perceived value is the same in both cases? Different? Why or why not?

3. What do you think the teachers can do to improve this situation? What would you do if you were one of the teachers? The parent?

4. How did the story make you feel about family engagement with socioeconomically disadvantaged families?

5. Do you see value in working toward a better relationship with this parent? Why or why not?

UNDERSTANDING THE IMPORTANCE OF RELATIONSHIPS WITH FAMILIES

Relationships between families and the schools that their children attend are complex. Often there is great ambiguity with regard to the differing interests of families and policies, procedures, and practices, and this ambiguity has an effect on the health of the relationship (Cullingford & Morrison, 1999). It is impossible to think that teachers can cultivate strong relationships with the students they teach, yet not create the very same strong relationships with their students' families.

However, when schools understand and nurture effective relationships with all families, tremendous dividends are paid in the form of achievement for every student. Karen Mapp (2003) summarizes it best:

> According to the parents, when school personnel initiate and engage in practices that welcome parents to the school, honor their contributions, and connect them to the school community through an emphasis on the children, these practices then cultivate and sustain respectful, caring, and meaningful relationships between parents and school staff. (p. 36)

Perceived value plays a huge role in whether or not relationships to support students will be fruitful.

No matter to what lengths we try and go to improve family engagement, without a real relationship built on trust and honesty, the efforts will probably fall short. If you do not honor all families and convey true appreciation for what they can bring to the partnership, regardless of their station in life, then those families will see through your efforts to engage them through a lens of skepticism.

Actions, attitudes, assumptions, beliefs, and values must all work together in order to build engagement with every family. And most importantly, when working with the disengaged, you must consider it really as working with one family at a time. Daunting? Yes. Impossible? No.

We cannot fix socioeconomic disparities, but we can convince every family, regardless of their station in life, that they have value and are truly needed to complete the circle of people that will successfully educate their children.

In a study conducted by Crozier and Davies (2007), the authors found that while parents were disengaged, they were by no means difficult, obstructive, or indifferent. Instead of labeling parents hard to reach, conclusions were that the schools themselves inhibited accessibility of these parents. It is common for schools to set policies and procedures that actually work against fostering relationships with all parents and then complain that parents and families are "hard to reach."

One could argue that it is a classic self-fulfilling prophecy. Relationships between schools and families are dependent on policies that have nothing to do with family engagement (Hallgarten, 2000). If family engagement is truly a priority for schools, then building successful relationships with all families should be at or near the top of the list of goals as opposed to being relegated to the deathly "if we have time."

Karen Mapp, Harvard University, has conducted extensive research in parent involvement and is the architect of "The Joining Process." Dr. Mapp is also one of the authors of *Beyond the Bake Sale: The Essential Guide to Family-School Partnerships* (Henderson et al., 2007). In the three-part Joining Process, the school community

1. Welcomes parents into the school

2. Honors their participation

3. Connects with parents through a focus on the children and their learning

Dr. Mapp and her colleagues provide ideas as catalysts for changes in practice and behavior by giving us items and ideas that support the concept of the joining process as well as items and ideas that may prevent the concept from taking shape in a school that wishes to engage every family. For example (Henderson et al., 2007):

Do More	Do Less
Hello! Welcome to our school. How may I help you?	Who are you? What do you want?
Welcome signs with name of the school and principals	NO TRESPASSING
Parent meetings that break into small discussion groups, each picking a leader	Parent meetings dominated by a few officers

It is clear that how we communicate and engage with families can either help or hinder our efforts to create a culture that welcomes and joins with every family. From the way families are greeted by our employees and signage, how and when we schedule, organize, and conduct meetings, how we value the contributions families make to our school or how we go about engaging them in new curriculum or instructional methodology, our approaches and attitudes will have a lot to do with our ultimate success.

There are many categories for us to consider when desiring to engage every family. A few have already been mentioned (communication, signage, meeting times and structures, and so forth.) What ideas do you have?

Create your own chart of "do more" and "do less" that you know will assist you in your efforts to engage every family. Think about additional categories other than those already mentioned. How do you solicit input and opinions? How do families learn of new programs and curricular initiatives? How do you promote parent/family leadership? How do you honor the role of families in the educational lives of their children? How do you celebrate achievement?

Do More	Do Less

(Continued)

(Continued)

Do More	Do Less

Source: Henderson et al., 2007.

Activity: Practices, Procedures, and Policies—Looking Through a Different Lens

How are relationships between your school and families helped or hindered by the practices, procedures, and policies that are implemented in your school? Look through the lens of every family and conduct a thorough inventory of practices, procedures, and policies to better understand how families are interpreting your school interactions.

Conduct a review of each category:

1. School/teacher/classroom policies, practices, and procedures: Determine if your practices and procedures are consistent and engaging to every family. Are there school-wide practices that hinder the ability of families to be engaged? Procedures and practices usually exist with everything from communication to homework to classroom visits to volunteerism.

2. With a group of colleagues, brainstorm a list of everything you can think of that can be considered a policy, practice, or procedure associated with your classrooms or school.

3. Once finished with a master list, group the items into different categories and label them.

4. As a staff, look at the categories and lists through the lens of families and consider how practices or policies could be changed or improved to engage every family.

TEACHER OUTREACH

Every family is not engaged. For the disengaged, there is an old adage that sums up how to reattach and reinvigorate relationships between families and schools:

Before they will come to you, you must go to them.

Outreach to families is an essential concept if a true desire exists to engage every family. Teacher outreach is an excellent way to build the relationships necessary to foster family engagement and to help those families that are disengaged become less fearful and more optimistic about the worth and value of their ability to engage.

But, and there is a big but here, it is impossible to ignore the fear and apprehension of teachers who are suddenly asked to reach out to families whom they may perceive as disengaged, unsupportive, disenfranchised, or difficult. Valuing teacher time is essential for outreach mechanisms to work. For many years, we have suggested that family engagement is not about doing more; it's about doing what we already do . . . just differently.

One of the biggest challenges to teacher outreach is time. Our teachers are incredibly busy and overburdened as it is. When the subject of outreach comes up, teachers are quick to ask "when?" It is important to remember that not all outreach involves time for teachers to work with families face-to-face—family engagement is not about doing more, it's about doing what we already do, just doing it differently. Here is one example of a change that takes no more time or effort but results in a very different outcome.

THE WEEKLY FOLDER

For as long as anyone can remember, elementary students have carried home a weekly folder. One day of the week is designated as "folder day." The students are given their folders and instructed to bring them home to share with their families. Students are told that the folder must come back to school the following day and a signature from a parent must be included.

Presumably, the parent signature is needed to ensure safe delivery of the information. Students clearly understand that they will only get one folder for the year and dire consequences could exist if the folder doesn't come back the next day!

Folders usually contain examples of work that has been done in school by the student as well as information for parents. The purpose of the weekly folder is noble: to communicate what is happening in school to parents and to give them examples of progress in learning as well as keep parents informed of school happenings.

Teachers spend a great deal of time preparing information for the weekly folder and rely on this method of communication to keep home–school information flowing. But does the folder meet the expected objectives? (We can debate using youngsters as conduits of communication at a later time!)

Let's look more closely at the folder and more importantly, look at ways in which the folder could be improved with no additional monies, effort, or time. Remember, family engagement is not about doing more . . . it's about doing things differently. One of the first salient questions is about engagement. How do we expect families to engage with things that have *already* happened? A folder full of information of what has already occurred leaves little or no opportunity for families to engage in learning.

The required signature is largely is so the teacher knows the families received the information she wished to communicate, and an adult caregiver viewed the information. In many cases, required signatures become a method of establishing proof of communication when families raise questions. Again, we need to ask a simple question: Does a signature mean that a parent has received the information or received and *understood* the information presented? Big difference.

In most cases, the signature cannot prove to the teacher the information was clearly communicated and understood. Is there a way then to change the weekly folder without adding any extra time or work for a teacher but to significantly increase its use and understanding by parents? The answer is simple: Yes.

Instead of using the folder to communicate what has occurred, change the focus to what *will* occur. What is happening in school tomorrow or next week, and how can parents support the teacher and their child's learning? Fill the folder with examples of what will be learned and how parents can extend the learning into the home. If a teacher feels strongly that examples of completed work are essential, then divide the folder in half. On the left side put a few examples of completed work, and on the right side place items that will be covered in the coming week.

Lastly, instead of a signature, why not pose a question instead? Let's say, for example, that students are studying dinosaurs as part of a science unit. Instead of a required signature, pose this question: "This week, we

studied dinosaurs and covered a lot of information. Ask your child what they have learned about dinosaurs and write down what they say here. Thank you."

Let's take an inventory of what we can accomplish with the same folder, the same resources, the same amount of time, but with a different focus:

1. Family support for home learning

2. Family understanding of concepts covered in school

3. Classroom learning extended into the home

4. Family efficacy for learning

5. The teacher's ability to check for conceptual understanding

No additional time. No additional resources. Just a change in what we do and how we do it. This simple change is but one of a number of examples of school practice and procedure that when slightly altered produce very different results.

It's important to note that in some schools, the weekly folder has been replaced by a modern day e-version. Whether information is shared on paper or on a web page or via e-mail, the goals are the same: to help families engage in the upcoming learning and to provide evidence of understanding of what has been shared.

Simple. Now, what else can we change? You knew that question was coming! Get together with some of your colleagues and start looking at time-tested practices that with a little updating could truly engage every family.

WORKING WITH THE "HARD TO REACH"

For a moment, let's ponder the label of the "hard-to-reach" parent. Did these parents and families label themselves? Did they arrive to our schools and announce that they are hard to reach so we should not bother to try? Perhaps there are a handful of parents who indicate that they cannot be reached or prefer not to be reached, but clearly they are a microscopic minority. The fact is that we educators have labeled parents "hard to reach" when they don't seem to conform to our perceptions of our standard communication protocols. However, they can be reached. It just takes knowing how and the willingness to make the necessary changes.

Often educators request strategies and ideas to communicate with these types of families. The first strategy is really not a strategy at all but harkens back to *Principle #1, A Culture that Engages Every Family.* The first and most important strategy is for us to believe that reaching out to these families has value and is worth our time and effort. If we don't believe that this effort has any benefit, then it is highly unlikely that we will see any results.

The second strategy is to embody the ethic of caring. In many cases, families who are disengaged or disenfranchised are often facing significant challenges in their personal lives. Stress from finances, work, and family take their toll on just about everyone but have a greater impact on those who may be less fortunate.

We should not judge these families or make assumptions about their support of their child's education. We need to understand the life situations that these families often find themselves in and let them know that all will be well and, more importantly, that partnering with them and building a relationship is something we welcome. We can convince them that regardless of their circumstances, together we can improve the outcomes for their children.

Thousands of studies have been written about the ability of socioeconomically disadvantaged students to learn, and those studies all indicate that, while there are obstacles, the students in this category are able to learn at rather impressive levels. Most of us are witness to numerous success stories of children with disadvantages rising up and beating the educational odds. In most cases, we shed preconceived notions and stereotypes about the children, their families, and their ability to learn. This is the third important strategy when looking to engage the hard-to-reach family. Keep an open mind about the family, regardless of who they are and where they live.

Ron Edmonds, the late researcher and father of the Effective Schools Movement, is credited with coining the phrase "all children can learn." A cornerstone idea in Effective Schools is the setting of high expectations for all students. Many have argued that leaving this one concept out of the equation has supported the achievement gaps that still plague education today. The fourth strategy in working with the hard-to-reach is to set high expectations for the relationship. Believe that the family cares about their child. Believe that they have the capacity to support learning at home, and believe that they really want to.

Lastly, be sensitive to the needs of families. Provide plenty of advance notice of meetings and multiple reminders. Everyone leads a busy life. One communication about a meeting is likely to get lost in a sea of other information. When offering important events, offer them more than once, on various days, and at various times. Give families more than one option for participation. Provide information for those who cannot attend and look for alternative meeting sites that are not in the school.

Activity: Event Location Planner

In many schools, there seems to be an unwritten law demanding that every meeting take place in the school library or cafeteria. This activity is designed to open the door to hosting school-related meetings at nonschool locations. Use the following chart to determine how events and activities at your school can subscribe to the notion of family outreach.

In the first column, list all of the activities, events, meetings, conferences, and so forth, which are presently hosted at your school. Include EVERYTHING. If you think you should not add something . . . add it! In the second column, determine if the activity can be moved from the school to another venue (i.e., does the PTA meeting have to be in the library?). If you determine there is an opportunity to move the activity/event, then determine possible locations within your community. An example is given to stimulate your thinking.

Event/Activity/ Meeting/Conference	Can It Be Moved From the School?	If So, What Are Some Potential Locations?
Parent conferences	Yes	Local library/apartment complex meeting room; community conference room at Walmart

(Continued)

(Continued)

Event/Activity/Meeting/Conference	Can It Be Moved From the School?	If So, What Are Some Potential Locations?

Source: Used with permission of Dr. Joni Samples, Family Friendly Schools. Chart is available for download at www.drsteveconstantino.com

HOME VISITS

In many workshops, I usually ask veteran teachers if they remember a time when home visits were part of the established routine for teachers. Every time I ask, the answer is the same: Yes. Teachers who have been around for a while remember home visits and even admit that they "used to do them." My next question, though, rarely gets answered: "Why did you stop?"

The words *home visits* often strike fear in the hearts of teachers. We cannot imagine that we have the time in our day to visit the homes of students and their families. Furthermore, teachers point to the safety and risk factors of home visits as another reason for avoiding this outreach strategy. However, as we have already learned earlier, there is an old adage that frames engaging the disengaged: "Before they will come to you, you must go to them." This strategy delivers strong results but takes time, patience, and some professional development to ensure success. However, it is simple!

Programs that provide time and funding for teachers to visit students and families on their own turf are a way for teachers to learn more about their students, get the families more involved in their children's education, and bridge cultural gaps that may be in place between student and teacher. Teachers who participate in home visits report them having a lasting effect on the child, the family, and parent-teacher communication.

Teachers' visits to students' homes can take many forms. The visitation approach might vary from school to school and from teacher to teacher. The approach might also depend on the funding source. In some schools, teachers prefer to travel in pairs to their visits; they feel more comfortable that way, and sometimes teachers need a translator in order to communicate with a child's parents. Other teachers visit one-on-one with parents. Some interact with the child and the parents. They bring along learning activities for the child that also involve a parent's participation. Visits can last anywhere from thirty to ninety minutes, depending on the teacher and the activities.

Arranging the visits, though, can require some creative scheduling. Teachers report that sometimes it can be a challenge to find a mutually agreeable time for a home visit. Some teachers go to the workplace of the parent if the parent is not able to be home during the day or early evening.

Many teachers report they were uncomfortable at first with the idea of visiting their students' homes, but most of those discomforts seem to dissipate once the actual visits begin. If parents are uncomfortable with the idea of a home visit, they are invited to meet the teacher at school or at another location. Encouraging parents to become more involved in their child's education by opening their homes to teacher visits has brought positive results to many schools and teachers who have tried it.

One note of caution: While teachers love home visits, it is wise to set them up for success with the proper professional development. Home visits require some skill and knowledge on the part of the teacher and the administration to implement a successful program. Effective programs prepare teachers to make a relationship, bring what they've learned back to the classroom, and apply it to the child's academic progress.

The Parent-Teacher Home Visit Project (PTHVP), originating in Sacramento, California, has spread across the United States as one of the most successful training models for teachers to prepare for effective home visits. A departure from typical assessment or disciplinary home visit programs, this model is specifically designed for teachers and parents to come together as equal partners, building trust, accountability, and cultural respect. Consistent with the research that shows that family engagement makes a difference in secondary school outcomes, PTHVP conducts high school and college readiness visits as well as K–8 (Carrie Rose, personal correspondence, February 2, 2015).

Quick Tip: Professional Development for Home Visits

The Parent Teacher Home Visit Project website has resources regarding effective home visits and contact information for its affiliates in over 17 states. Visit their site at http://www.pthvp.org.

WORKING WITH FAMILIES WITH LIMITED ENGLISH PROFICIENCY

Questions about engaging the hard-to-reach family can quickly turn to the challenges associated with families with limited English proficiency. The basic strategies listed above are universal and can be applied with any category of disengaged family. However, there are factors to consider and specific strategies to employ to improve relationships with families with limited English proficiency.

It should come as no surprise that the first principle to apply in working with these families has its roots in culture. Exploring, learning, and valuing family beliefs are important foundations when working with families with limited English proficiency. The more we can learn and value the customs of particular cultures, the greater the likelihood that we can create relationships built on respect and trust.

Often schools run up against expectation barriers placed by families based on a number of factors. For example, families feel judged by their occupation, economic status, and social group. Their self-esteem is low because of assimilation issues with regard to their new culture. Their children adapt to U.S. customs far faster than their families. Understand that many first-generation immigrant families are experiencing a kind of culture shock upon which schooling adds another dimension.

Communication is a key factor in working with families with limited English proficiency. Understand the differences between formal and informal communication and the differences in perception of face-to-face conversations and telephone conversations of the cultures with which you are working. In most cases, community leaders can help educators understand the nuances of culture and custom and how to apply the best communication methods available.

Families will feel more comfortable in connecting with a school if orientation sessions in native languages are provided for families. Allowing families to form parent groups based on culture and language may seem antithetical to our inclusive philosophy; however, research shows that these groups actually help families acclimate to the culture of the school and make the transition to established school groups smoother and more successful.

COMMUNITY-BASED PTA MODEL

A small but growing phenomenon is taking shape in communities in Texas and may be expanding to other states and localities as well, especially those where many families are disadvantaged, might speak Spanish, and are recent immigrants to the United States. The community-based PTA movement is a way to meaningfully engage families who are often left out.

For example, in a community in Texas, a group of about twenty families got together and discussed forming their own *community-based* official PTA unit. Most were fluent only in Spanish, and all were poor. The schools their children attended were either academically challenged or feeders to low-achieving secondary schools. At the initial meeting, the parents shared their reasons for wanting a PTA and compared their opinions with those of the national PTA available in Spanish on the website. They confirmed that their vision was congruent with that of the national organization.

The Intercultural Development Research Association (IDRA) has been around for over 40 years and is a leader in helping to support meaningful family engagement through community-based PTAs. Working hand in hand with a Texas Parent Involvement Resource Center (PIRC), IDRA has been a catalyst in helping these families garner a voice in the education of their children, and it seems to be paying off.

IDRA spokesman Aurelio M. Montemayor, MEd, discusses these community organizations using data to improve learning and schools. He tells the story of a group of low-income Spanish-speaking families and their high school children using data and surveys to collaborate with their school to improve math instruction. "If data is presented in meaningful chunks, parents will look at it, will ask the right questions and, if supported and encouraged, will take steps to at least dig deeper in a way that will help the school understand" (Montemayor, personal communication, December 22, 2014).

> **For More Information . . .**
>
> To get more information on the community PTA movement and the work being done with ARISE, visit the IDRA website at http://www.idra.org/IDRA_Family_Center/.

Family engagement in the United States is vastly different than family engagement in other countries. In some countries, the concept is completely foreign. The school is an extension of the state government, and parents play no role in the education of their children. Upon arrival to the United States, these families are suddenly faced with our family engagement expectations, which they simply do not understand.

Often, when families stay away and do not respond to schools, they are doing what they believe to be correct and expected. Educators must exercise patience when establishing these relationships. It simply will take some time . . . but it is not difficult. In fact, it is quite simple!

ENGAGING WITH FAMILIES OF CHILDREN WITH SPECIAL NEEDS

Most of the time we desire tangible evidence of family engagement. We want to know that families participate in events we host or that they have reviewed information we send to them. The evidence produced from these kinds of interactions helps us to know that our efforts are assisting with improved communication and, perhaps more importantly, the self-efficacy of families.

Families of children with special needs often devote a great deal more time to ensuring the success of their children, both in and out of school. Engaging the families of children with special needs provides a unique set of challenges. Between individualized education program (IEP) meetings, required accommodations to student learning plans, the requirement to inform families of their due process rights, and so forth, there is a significant amount of engagement already inherent in the relationship. Or is there?

Interestingly, with all of these opportunities for interaction, families of students with special needs report less interaction with schools, because of the perceived barriers in engagement (Rodriguez, Blatz, & Elbaum, 2014). Even though there is often more established contact between families of students with special needs and schools, levels of family engagement when compared to general education students remained about the same (Derubetis & Yanok, 1989). Deslandes et al. (1999) suggest that families with children with special needs may hold the perception that they are less likely, capable, or able to have an impact on their child's academic life and as such tend to be less engaged.

Different Degrees of Family Engagement
for Families of Children With Special Needs

In their study, Rodriguez, Blatz, & Elbaum (2014) discovered themes within the context of the engagement of families of children with special needs. For example, families that spoke positively about the school's ability and desire to collaborate frequently mentioned the accessibility of teachers and more importantly that teachers and families could openly disagree without being disagreeable. Families who spoke unfavorably about this theme pointed to the rigidity of staff members and the need to go higher up the chain of command to resolve issues.

Families of children with special needs are very much in tune with the academic progress of their children and the extent to which the school provides necessary support for success. Properly trained teachers, competency, and choice were all ideas presented by families who spoke favorably about their child's school and the progress their child was making. The death knell, it seems, is the perception of families that some teachers were "unfamiliar with their children's IEP" (Rodriguez, Blatz, & Elbaum, 2014, p. 87).

Families of students with special needs believe that it is important for them to be persistent with regard to the services their children need. Families of children with special needs will take initiative and action regardless or in spite of a school's failure to engage them. These families desire the school to facilitate their engagement in the education of their children (Rodriguez, Blatz, and Elbaum, 2014).

Families of children with special needs identify three characteristics of communications they deem positive: (1) communications that occur regularly, (2) communication that is focused on the child's progress, and (3) communication that allows a variety of methods of interaction (Rodriguez, Blatz, and Elbaum, 2014). Families often speak of differences from year to year with regard to changes in personnel at school. The inconsistency from teacher to teacher translates into parental concern on the part of the school to care for thier children. Family views of schools' efforts to engage them are directly connected to their views of the quality of the education and services that are provided to their children.

Consider this scenario: A parent or family member arrives to an IEP meeting. She walks into the meeting and sees numerous people seated around a table—a teacher, the special education teacher, a counselor, a psychologist, an administrator, and, depending on the specific plan, other types of support staff. The parent is told what will occur, and then, after everyone speaks at her, she is asked to sign a form about the IEP for her child. If she disagrees with the IEP or refuses to sign it, a sheet of paper with her rights is handed to her.

Perhaps this example is exaggerated; perhaps it is not. The processes associated with students with special needs can be daunting to families. It's no wonder why the level of family engagement seems to be somewhat extreme—either extremely involved with advocates and lawyers or extremely disengaged with educational processes designed to improve student learning. Brinckerhoff and Vincent (1986) suggested in their research that IEP processes were not good examples of two-way communication.

Families of children with special needs support and work with their children every moment the children are not in school. Depending on the disability, it can be both daunting and exhausting for these families. More often than not, when contacted by the school, they receive negative information and rarely perceive they are treated as equal partners in the education of their children. All of this mixed together spells disaster for engaging all of these families.

The answers to these issues are many and perhaps could be a book by themselves. In the quest to keep it simple, let's look at some high-return ideas to improve the engagement of families with special needs children:

- Provide parent/staff training in writing developmental assessments: When assessing a child's developmental level, it will be beneficial to have parents understand how these processes occur.
- Promote professional development for teachers in how to participate in a meeting and how to establish priorities.
- Create welcoming physical environments in meeting rooms and special education areas.
- Assign a parent liaison to meet and greet families, understand their needs and expectations, explain to families what to expect, and reinforce to families that the school is interested in their views.

CASE STUDY: JONATHAN AND THE SELF-CONTAINED ENGLISH CLASS

Elizabeth Wood is a seasoned special education teacher and by all accounts one of the finest teachers at R. D. Lynch High School. Both the administration and her colleagues respect the work that she does and the knowledge that she brings to educating children with special needs. Elizabeth embraces students with disabilities and is the one who always offers to take on the most challenging teaching assignments. Her success rate in student learning is unmatched.

Jonathan Downey has been assigned to Elizabeth's self-contained English 9 class. There are nine students in the classroom and all of them are challenged with various behavioral disorders. Jonathan has a history of school failure and has a pattern of disruptive behavior in school. His school experiences have been negative almost since the day he entered kindergarten. Jonathan's mother, Valerie, is committed to Jonathan's success and has been an engaged parent and a champion for her son despite her own adverse experiences in school. She has experienced her share of setbacks and issues with Jonathan and is adept at navigating school bureaucracy to advocate for her son.

Prior to the first day of class, Elizabeth contacted the families of each of the nine students in her self-contained classroom. She introduced herself and had the simple goal of establishing a positive relationship with the families of the students in her classes. Skeptical of the call, Valerie quizzed Elizabeth about classroom procedures and expectations. Elizabeth skillfully answered the questions but kept the focus on the need to build a trusting relationship between school and home.

Jonathan arrived to class on the first day exhibiting the behaviors that had caused him issues for most of his education. He behaved immaturely and was unable to control his outbursts in class. He was not a danger to classmates but was clearly disruptive to the learning environment for himself and others. Elizabeth's first assignment was for each of the students to create an autobiographical collage to share with the class. Elizabeth faced a significant challenge in getting Jonathan to focus on the assignment; however, she was able to learn from the pictures he chose that Jonathan was an avid basketball fan and enjoyed computers.

After a few days of disruptive behavior, Elizabeth called Valerie again. In the conversation, Elizabeth did not mention the poor classroom behaviors exhibited by Jonathan but rather focused on what she had learned about Jonathan's learning style and the environment in which she believed he would flourish. Elizabeth shared with Valerie the things she would do to support Jonathan in class. Valerie waited for the negative comments about her son, but they never came.

Each week, the calls were the same. Elizabeth reached out to Valerie to inform her of the progress Jonathan was making, even though his behaviors and outbursts were continuing. Jonathan would arrive home and his mother would inform him that Ms. Wood called her. Fearing the worst, Jonathan would begin to defend himself only to find out that Ms. Wood had nothing but praise for the progress Jonathan was making.

After five weeks of school, Jonathan's behaviors in class markedly improved. He was attentive and significantly less disruptive. He started to emerge as a class leader and even learned to raise his hand instead of blurting out answers or off-task comments. Elizabeth never wrote a referral for Jonathan's behavior. She simply continued to keep lines of communication open with Jonathan's mother and continued to reward and praise the behavior that was expected in her classroom.

During a conference at the end of the nine-week grading period, Valerie commented to Elizabeth that for the first time in her experience with the school system, Jonathan was not being disciplined or suspended from class. She shared that Jonathan still seemed to have problems in other classes that resulted in disciplinary interventions and loss of instructional time that would never be recovered. Elizabeth worked with Valerie on strategies to help Jonathan be as successful in other classrooms as he was in English 9. Valerie ended the conversation by saying "Jonathan just adores you . . . and so do I. Thank you for believing in my son."

Questions for Discussion

1. Can you think of situations that you have been in where students like Jonathan have created a difficult classroom environment? How did you react?

2. Why do you think that Elizabeth never mentioned the difficulties she was experiencing in class with regard to Jonathan's behaviors?

3. What do you think Elizabeth deems most important when working with a student like Jonathan?

4. What was Elizabeth's goal in reaching out to Valerie?

5. Why do you think Jonathan's behaviors improved in Elizabeth's class but did not improve in other classes?

6. Thinking about the Five Simple Principles, which were at work to help Jonathan be successful?

Activity: Changing Practices and Procedures to Improve Outreach and Increase Family Engagement

The chart below is designed to get you thinking about procedures and practices that are in place that, when slightly altered, could become more effective in promoting outreach and family engagement. The example of "the folder" is one of many examples that can be altered and enhanced. A few ideas are provided to stimulate your thinking.

Original Procedure or Practice	Redesigned Procedure or Practice	What Will It Take to Redesign?
Standard homework	Interactive homework (homework that has a component for parent participation or understanding)	Change in how homework is constructed (no new time) Change in types of assignments (no new resources)
Remediation	Home learning support	Design resources for both parents and students (no new resources, no new time). Share concepts of student learning with parents.
PTA meetings	PTA meetings that promote family efficacy and learning	Each PTA meeting has a learning component for parents (no new time, no new money, no new resources).

Original Procedure or Practice	Redesigned Procedure or Practice	What Will It Take to Redesign?

Disengaged families do not immediately respond to outreach efforts. Remember, we still have to work on fear, trust, and relationships. But don't be discouraged—every effort is a step in the right direction!

Chart is available for download at www.drsteveconstantino.com

THE ROLE OF FEAR AND TRUST IN RELATIONSHIPS WITH FAMILIES

There can be no relationship without trust. Often, disengaged families are distrusting of the school system (see Chapter 3). Either they have had experiences with their children that have been negative, or they hearken back to their own experience that planted the seeds of mistrust years before their own children attended school.

Whether or not there was ever a time when families unconditionally trusted teachers and educators is hard to say. What is easier to say is there is a need in today's society to work toward building trust between home and school. We simply live in a different world, a world that is dominated by anonymity and insecurity. Building trusting relationships with every family will go a long way to negate the ills we face.

What actions promote distrust between schools and families? The following lists are by no means exclusive. The items below represent the more common actions that promote distrust between schools and families.

School Actions That Can Promote Mistrust

- *Inaccurate information, out-of-date information, or lack of information on school websites or in other forms of communication.*
- *Teacher websites that are unused or not updated.* Many schools have added teacher websites as another means to promote communication. Unfortunately, with inconsistent use, these items work almost in the opposite fashion than intended.
- *Lack of follow through* (promises not kept, mistakes in grading left unattended, important information not corrected, etc.).
- *Practices and procedures that are limiting to families* (no-visit policies, no volunteers needed, etc.).
- *Discipline issues.* Often a lack of understanding, perceived unfairness, or disagreement with discipline can play a significant role in parental mistrust of schools.
- *Lack of involvement in decisions.* School districts, schools, and classrooms often make decisions without involving or engaging stakeholders in the process.

Parental Actions That Promote Mistrust

- *Sporadic attendance patterns of children.* Educators become skeptical and suspicious of families where there are attendance issues. Educators tend to believe it is the parents' responsibility for the child to attend school.
- *Defensive posture toward school actions.* Some parents continuously defend the actions of their children and hold the school accountable for all situations.
- *Lack of response to school-initiated communication.* School personnel quickly become skeptical of parents when letters or e-mails go unanswered or phone calls are not returned.
- *Defensive or threatening responses to school communication.*
- *Non-attendance to school functions designed for parents and families.* Many families do not attend school functions or conferences, leaving a great deal of doubt in the minds of educators as to their commitment toward their children's learning
- *Aggressive actions toward the school.* Whether storming the main office and demanding an audience with the principal, public displays of aggression in meetings or assemblies, or sending tersely worded e-mails, aggressive behavior by parents often leads to distrustful relationships.

Questions for Discussion

1. Have any of the items in the lists above ever happened in your school?
2. Can you think of other actions or behaviors that promote mistrust?

mean the person disagrees but rather is seeking clarification the best way they know how. Dialog promotes understanding and support.

THE WELCOMING ENVIRONMENT OF SCHOOLS

One does not have to look far to find a large amount of literature devoted to the notion of a welcoming environment in schools. Often, this concept is the easiest for schools to check off their to-do lists, placing welcome signs, directional signs, and so forth. While these efforts are certainly important to the welcoming environment of schools, it is the attitude of the personnel within the school that will either support a welcoming environment or clearly send messages to parents that welcoming signs are window dressing.

A common complaint among families is a lack of a welcoming environment of their child's school. They report feeling as if they are imposing or interrupting when they visit the school. Because of the need for increased security, they often are buzzed into the school and questioned about the reason for their visit. In larger, more complex schools, finding the correct door (usually only one is unlocked, if any) and finding their way can be daunting. Even though they appreciate the attention to safety and security, once inside they are somewhat intimidated not only by the complexity of an environment that seems foreign to them but also a less-than-warm reception from school employees.

Activity: Getting to the Destination

Here is a simple activity that not only can underscore the experiences families have when arriving to our schools but can actually begin to create an inventory of needs to make the school more welcoming.

Go outside and move to the edge of the school property. Pretend that you have never been to the school before. Ask yourself: Can I get where I want to go? Are the entrances clearly marked? Are there signs directing me to the office or guest area? Are there people who can assist? As a guest who has never been to the school before, can I find my way to my destination?

Now, repeat the process above, only this time, in addition to pretending that you have never been to the school before, also pretend that you neither speak nor understand English. Now, ask yourself the same question again: Can I get to where I want to go?

Taking a few minutes to participate in this activity can completely change your perceptions of the welcoming environment of your school and help you begin to change those systems that will ultimately help to engage every family.

CUSTOMER SERVICE

Like it or not, public education is quickly becoming a commodity. For a very long time, maybe since the inception of public schools, educators have not seen themselves as having to convince customers of the quality of their product. Today, that has all changed. With the rise of alternatives to the public school setting, the way we think, behave, market, and conduct our business will define our future success.

Consider for a moment the rapid development of online learning platforms. In the last few years, the use of online learning has sky-rocketed. An increasing number of states now require students to have at least one online learning experience as a component of successful graduation, and on-line high schools are here now. Online learning uses resources and teachers very differently and is already significantly altering everything from school scheduling to teacher contracts. There are many who note that the advent of online learning can save money traditionally devoted to teacher salaries. In effect, it could put us out of business, if some get their way.

Every business in the private sector understands the basic tenets of doing business: customer requirements. Find out what the needs of the customer are and then provide the product or solution to meet the customer's needs. The better the company and product, the more likely the sale. Educators will be well served to adopt this philosophy of thinking.

As important as customer requirements are, so is customer service. The service that we provide before, during, and after the "sale" of our product will be strategic in our efforts to maintain a healthy market share. There are some basic principles of customer service that are important to understand and incorporate into all we do.

First and foremost, we must be good at what we do. Greeting people warmly and with a genuine smile and caring attitude is important, but being good at what we do is essential, otherwise we are not providing the kind of service expected by our customer. We must model excellence, always.

Follow-through and trustworthiness are essential to quality services. We need to do what we say we will do and always try to exceed expectations of our customers. Simple things like making and returning phone calls in a timely fashion pay huge dividends with families. Scheduling meetings at a convenient time for families and ensuring we are in attendance may seem like a small token, but the message these efforts send is a resounding "we care."

Our students and their families must always feel respected and well cared for. Each family, regardless of their background or preconceived notion, must instinctively sense our desire to make an important personal connection with them, to value their role in the educational partnership, and to support the notion that they are important.

(Continued)

had made the rules clear and the rules were not followed. He then indicated that it was common for students who did not finish assignments to say they handed them in. The conversation became heated, and Susan's parents left very upset, vowing to call the superintendent's office.

Study #2 The Fight

Joey and his friend Alan had a falling out. The next day during lunch, Joey and Alan met up again. This time, Joey pushed Alan and Alan fell to the ground. Joey tried to punch Alan, but another student intervened. Alan did not strike Joey but did antagonize him, causing Joey to become angry.

The assistant principal suspended both boys from school for three days for fighting. Joey's parents did not contest the discipline. Alan's parents, however, believed that because Alan did not strike Joey back or hit Joey first, Alan should be spared the suspension. The school cited their student discipline code and indicated that Alan provoked the fight with his words. Further, the assistant principal indicated that there was no time to "sort out who did what to whom," and thus, the suspension stood. Alan's parents were upset and headed to their attorney's office.

Study #3 The School Visit

John was an elementary school student. John's mother speaks little English and, even though she attends all of his conferences and meetings, does not clearly understand all that is being presented to her. Because she came to this country to do the best she could for her children, she is always compliant and never argues or questions the school. In her country, one does not question the school.

John began to decline academically and behaviorally. John's mother understood that her son was having problems in school but didn't know what to do to help him. John also became more problematic at home. John's mother, being a single parent and raising three children, was at her wit's end with John and decided to go to the school for help.

When she arrived, she found the doors of the school locked. The sign with the instructions to get into the school was in English, and she could not understand how to enter the school. She banged on the door until someone passing by let her into the school. She asked for help in her native language, but the person opening the door shrugged his shoulders in an "I do not know" gesture and continued to walk toward his destination.

John's mother walked into the first office she saw, which happened to be the security office. There she tried to explain her situation to a woman behind the desk. The woman indicated that she did not understand and motioned John's mother to follow her. The woman led her to the main office and motioned for her to sit down. She told

3. What strategies can we employ to reduce these issues and thus build more trusting relationships with every family?

CASE STUDIES

Each of the studies is a short vignette designed to help you think through the process of building relationships and trust with every family. The purpose of reading the studies and reflecting on the questions is not to determine right or wrong but to determine a different process that may have led to a different outcome, hopefully one that builds trusting relationships. For each of the case studies, answer the following questions:

1. What could the school personnel have done to help this situation end better for all involved?

2. What could the parent(s) have done to help this situation end better for all involved?

3. What kind of relationship do you think the parents had with the school before the issue? What do you think will happen to the relationship now that the issue has occurred?

4. Why did the circumstances happen the way they did? What insights do you have into the culture of the school in each of the studies?

5. What role does trust play in the case study?

Study #1 The Project

A middle school teacher designed a four-week project for students to complete. The project had a deadline, and the teacher made it clear to students there would be no negotiation: Late or missing assignments would be treated with a significantly reduced grade. On the day of the assignment, Susan, a student, turned it in as instructed. She vividly recalls handing the assignment to the teacher. Susan is an excellent student with good grades and no behavior issues at school.

The next day, the teacher asked Susan where her assignment was. Susan indicated she had handed it in. The teacher refuted Susan's claim and told her, "If you handed it in, I would have it." Susan went home upset and explained the issue to her parents. Both of her parents escorted her to school the next morning in hopes that they could speak to the teacher and sort it out.

Susan's parents were told the teacher was unavailable, and they were going to have to speak to the principal. They agreed. After waiting about fifteen minutes, they were ushered into the principal's office. They explained the situation to the principal. The principal indicated that he was not going to step into the situation. The teacher

(Continued)

the office secretary that she didn't understand what John's mother's problem was and it would be better if someone in the main office talked with her. The secretary and the woman from security talked for a few more minutes about unrelated matter while John's mother waited in her seat.

About twenty minutes went by, and the principal approached John's mother and extended his hand to greet her. She said "hello." The principal only spoke English and could only say in his second language that he did not speak the second language John's mother tried to share her concerns about John, but the communication between the principal and John's mother was poor. John's mother began to cry. The principal indicated that John was a good boy and was doing fine in school. John's mother thanked the principal for his time and left the school. She cried uncontrollably after exiting the school.

IDEAS TO PROMOTE TRUSTING RELATIONSHIPS BETWEEN SCHOOLS AND EVERY FAMILY

Henderson et al. (2007) make the following point about school-family relationships: "When school staff construct caring and trustful relationships with parents, treating parents as partners in their children's education, parents are far more likely to become involved and stay involved" (p. 47). Educators instinctively know that relationships are important but struggle to figure out ways to actually make these relationships really work.

Much of the information on building relationships centers on making schools welcoming to families. Later in this chapter, we'll explore the ideas of welcoming environments more closely. First, let's test what you believe about engaging every family.

Determine whether or not you concur with the following statements. Record your answers.

1. Every family, regardless of their station in life, can make a contribution toward their children's education. (Agree or Disagree)

2. Parents should have a voice in the education of their children. (Agree or Disagree)

3. Parents should have a voice in selecting teachers for their children. (Agree or Disagree)

4. It is important to include difficult parents in school decisions. (Agree or Disagree)

5. Respecting parent points of view is essential to successfully educating their children. (Agree or Disagree)

6. It is important to build a relationship with every family. (Agree or Disagree)

7. I fear talking with some families. (Agree or Disagree)

8. Parents should be allowed to visit classrooms anytime they wish. (Agree or Disagree)

9. Helping parents guide their children's learning is as important as teaching the children. (Agree or Disagree)

10. Every family has value. (Agree or Disagree)

Each of the statements above reflects a value statement that supports the ideas presented in Principle #2 regarding the importance of building relationships. There is no sliding scale to determine where your attitude is regarding effectively building relationships with families. For those statements with which you disagree, spend some time reflecting on why. Discuss these ideas with colleagues. Remember, what we believe and value shapes our attitudes and assumptions. As our actions and thoughts change so then does the culture of our organization.

Patterson, Grenny, McMillan, & Switzler (2012) indicate that a crucial conversation is one that can best be described as any day-to-day conversation in which the outcome is critical or crucial to long-term success. A key ingredient in building relationships with families is understanding the importance of communication and conversations that are open, honest, and a true exchange of ideas. One-sided conversations, talking without listening, talking down to parents, or simply putting everything in an e-mail are surefire ways to either destroy relationships or never build them in the first place.

A significant challenge to building relationships is one-way communication flow. Schools that send things home and do not invite return information, comment, or engagement chip away at the very foundation of needed relationships. (The ideas presented in "The Folder" activity combat this problem too!)

Teachers often report a fear of building relationships with every family. Most of the time, this fear is built upon experiences. If a teacher's interactions with families are largely negative, then it stands to reason that their opinions of building relationships and engaging with families will also be negative.

The solution lies in devoting some professional development time to working effectively with families and communication training. In order to do so, however, we must see the connection between engaging every family and student learning outcomes. We must value relationships with families as an express conduit to improved academic performance in all children.

We often mistake silence for acceptance and negative responses or dialog as a sign of disagreement. Actually, the reverse is also true. Silence could very well speak to an individual's frustration with a system and their loss of hope in terms of believing they can effect any positive change. A disagreeable person who is questioning or arguing does not necessarily

Let's ask this important question again: If all families truly had a choice in the schools to which they would send their children, would they choose yours? In other words, what differentiates your school from the other schools and options that are and increasingly will be open to families? Could placing a high value on family relationships set you apart from your competition? How far beyond common expectations are you willing to go in order to gain and keep customers?

Every day, we have problems and challenges in our business. We are a people business, and most of what we do centers on the interaction of humans. We cannot avoid the daily challenges that come with educating children. However, how we interact with our customer, how we handle and respond to the challenges we face, and the consistency with which we develop relationships with families will ultimately dictate our success.

BASIC CUSTOMER SERVICE TIPS TO GET YOU STARTED

Creating and sustaining a welcoming environment in your school is probably the lowest hanging fruit with regard to engaging every family. It is simple, doesn't cost any money, and the implementation can begin tomorrow. Following are a couple of ideas to get you going.

The Ten-Second Rule. When someone enters your school or office, do not let him or her wait for more than ten seconds before they are acknowledged. Even a "Thank you for coming today. Please be patient, I'll be with you in a few minutes," is better than nothing or a stiff "Just a minute."

The Telephone Answer. Yes, there is most definitely something important in how the telephone is consistently answered in your school. Create a greeting to which everyone will subscribe. "It's a great day at (Name) School. My name is _____. How can I help you?" Try it. It works. The attitude people have toward your organization will improve.

The Warm Transfer. There is nothing more annoying to any of us than calling an organization, explaining our question or concern, and then being transferred to another person, only to start our story over again. The warm transfer is an old business technique that requires the caller to explain their concern, question, or problem once. If the person answering the phone cannot help, they keep the caller on the line, secure the person that can help, then put the caller and the new person together on the line. The dialog can be as simple as this: "Mr. Jones, I have John on the line, and I have explained your concern to him. He is going to take it from here, because he is the person who can help you. Is there anything else I can do for you today? Thank you for calling." This little technique pays huge dividends to organizations wishing to improve perception and customer loyalty.

CEO Check-Ins. Every day, schools get calls from families with concerns or questions. Keep a log of those calls. At the end of a week, the CEO should pick two or three of those calls and call the parent or family member who originally called with a concern. The CEO can simply ask if the problem was resolved or not and reinforce to the parent the school or district commitment to resolving conflicts. A follow-up call from the head of the organization will leave a lasting, positive impression, regardless of the outcome of the original concern.

A Simple Thank-You. As education becomes more and more of a commodity, try this idea. It could very well alter the trajectory of your success. Have every member of the organization make a phone call to a parent or family member for no other reason than to say this: "I wanted to call today to let you know how much I enjoy having your son/daughter in my classroom. We value your child and you. Thank you for choosing to attend (school/district)." The purpose of the call is nothing more than to reinforce that you do not take a parent's choice for granted. Start this. It will make a difference.

A Simple and Effective Welcome

More and more businesses are providing staff members to greet and welcome customers. From saying hello, handing you a shopping cart, or providing you with the daily specials, the use of greeters is seen as an effective way to make customers feel welcome.

Different companies have different techniques, from the simple to the attention grabbing. One of the most notable is the greeting one gets upon arriving to Moe's Southwestern Grill. Upon opening the door, every employee behind the counter stops whatever they are doing and yells, "Welcome to Moe's!" They are consistent from customer to customer and restaurant to restaurant. Everyone who goes to Moe's knows of this famous welcoming greeting. The next time you find yourself near a Moe's, try stopping by!

How do you welcome guests to your school?

WELCOMING EVERY FAMILY

The chart below offers you an opportunity to consider those items known to increase the welcoming environments of schools. The chart acts as an action plan of sorts to determine what is in place and what needs to be improved. Get a group of colleagues together to review the chart. Then, ask families and students their opinions as well. Sometimes our perceptions as educators are very different from those of the families and students we serve.

Questions for Consideration	Present Conditions	Necessary or Desired Outcomes	Things to Be Done to Achieve Desired Outcomes	Notes, Questions, etc.
Do your school entrances welcome every family?				
Are entrances clearly marked and understandable by all?				
Are security measures clearly posted and communicated to all families?				
Are your faculty, student, and community parking well marked and understandable by all?				
Is handicapped parking clearly marked?				
Are handicapped entrances accessible and clearly marked?				
Are the parking lots and entrances well lit?				
If graffiti appears at your school, is it promptly removed?				
Is the interior of your school clean and well kept?				
Do families perceive your school as being safe?				
Does your school have a standing school beautification committee?				

(Continued)

Questions for Consideration	Present Conditions	Necessary or Desired Outcomes	Things to Be Done to Achieve Desired Outcomes	Notes, Questions, etc.
Does your school building contain understandable directional signs?				
Is there a comfortable reception area for families?				
Does your school have a parent/family center?				
Is your school administration approachable by all families?				
Does your school provide translation services for families who do not speak English?				
Must families ask for translation or is the service evident upon arrival?				
Does your school minimize the use of educational jargon?				
Do staff members treat families courteously?				
Does your school have an engaging website?				
Does your school use social media tools to communicate and welcome families?				

Source: Used with permission of Dr. Joni Samples, Family Friendly Schools. Chart is available for download at www.drsteveconstantino.com

Quick Tip: Helping Everyone Feel Welcome

For guests who do not speak English, it is often cumbersome and embarrassing to ask for translation. In many cases, the need to ask for translation deters non-English-speaking guests from coming to school. There are two easy solutions to this: (1) Find volunteers who speak the native language(s) in your school and make them a button that says "I speak (Language)" in the native language. Upon entering, a non-English-speaking guest is put at ease. (2) If volunteers are not available, place a decal or placard in the window or door of the entrances to the schools with the same message as above. Guests will know that someone speaks their language. These are two simple tips that go a long way toward establishing welcoming environments for everyone!

ISSUES AND SOLUTIONS IN COMMUNICATING WITH FAMILIES

Very little professional development time, if any at all, is devoted to helping teachers communicate with every family. The following section is designed to take issues and challenges in communicating with every family and provide practical solutions that can be implemented in a very simple fashion.

Issues in communication seem to be the ones that can anger both teachers and families and create tension, which hinders positive relationship building. Here are some tips and ideas to improve relationships with better communication:

1. *Major changes.* Don't make major instructional or curricular changes without either family input or notice. Changes to calendars, meetings, planned activities, and so forth, without sufficient notice or involvement leads to mistrust and animosity.

2. *Share information in a timely fashion.* The more quickly and thoroughly information is shared with families, the less likely families will be angry, rumors will swirl, and misconceptions will form.

3. *No surprises.* We don't like surprises. Neither do families.

4. *Don't make promises you can't keep.* If you indicate to a parent you will do something, then do it. Often we indicate we will do something or promise to do something and for a host of reasons do not follow through. This only breeds mistrust.

5. *The letter of the law and the spirit of the law.* Use common sense with issues that surround children and families. Don't overreach your authority to prove a point or hold your ground on a particular issue. Know the difference between policy and common sense.

6. *Don't label.* Never label parents by marital status, religious affiliation or beliefs, ethnicity, or socioeconomic status.

7. *Don't get defensive.* Remember that most of the messages parents have received over time are perceived to protect teachers and schools without regard to students and their families. Whether true or fair, the perception exists. Defensiveness is natural but unwise and is almost always perceived as guilt.

8. *Meetings.* Give parents a say in meeting calendars. Setting dates with no input and without checking for parent availability is unwise.

9. *Identify meeting purposes.* One of the most damaging things we can do to relationships with families is to set meetings with them and not let them know the purpose of the meeting.

10. *Physical and verbal barriers.* Using furniture, tables, or room setup to keep parents and school employees separated reinforces the notion that we do not value relationships with every family. Using sarcasm or belligerent or demeaning words or actions is never a good idea, regardless of the situation.

11. *Meeting participants held to a minimum.* Parents are often overwhelmed when they come to meetings and the room is filled with specialists and support personnel. If it is critical these people be at the meeting, contact the parent and let them know who will be at the meeting and their purpose for attending. Put them at ease that the meeting will be productive.

12. *Show up.* If you have a scheduled conference or meeting, attend. Don't send an e-mail or a grade sheet in your place.

13. *No blame.* When things don't go exactly right, don't point fingers and blame students, parents, the school, the administration, or other entities. Describe the challenge and work together to find solutions. It doesn't really matter how the problem started or who started it.

14. *Be trustworthy.* You cannot make people trust you, but you can earn the trust of anyone. Personal and professional behavior that withstands scrutiny and invites confidence goes a long way toward establishing healthy relationships with every family.

15. *Keep an open mind.* Don't prematurely judge people you do not know based on rumors or the comments made by others.

16. *Keep calm.* There are difficult people on the earth. Always remain calm. Remember the old saying "To change a difficult person, you must first change yourself."

17. *If you are wrong or make a mistake.* Admit it, apologize for it, and move on. Trying to avoid responsibility will not end well . . . for anyone.

18. *Do your homework.* When confronted with a meeting with a difficult or angry parent, find a piece of positive information about the parent, family, or student and use it to ease the tension.

19. *Think about responses.* If you are angered by a parent, use the "wait twenty-four hours" rule before responding. Never use e-mail and TYPE IN ALL CAPITALS. I call that "e-yelling."

20. *Demand strategy.* When a parent makes a demand that you cannot meet, do not say, "I cannot do that." Simply reiterate the things that you can do. After a few minutes, the strategy will have a calming effect and allow you an opportunity to enlist the parent's help in problem solving.

21. *Remember.* Anger is a mask for fear.

22. *Don't do these things.* Interrupt. Think about what you are going to say while the parent is talking. Change the subject. Focus on things that cannot be changed. Complain about your own agenda or situation. Embark in silent combat (stare down). Rehearse your answers before you have heard the question. Give advice unless you are asked. Persuade that you are right and they are wrong. Try so hard to be neutral that you show no empathy. Compulsively talk and overexplain. Lie. Let yourself get abused or bullied when sincerely trying to communicate.

CONNECTING COMMUNICATION AND RELATIONSHIPS WITH TECHNOLOGY

Employing strategies that extend relationship-building opportunities beyond the school walls so that every family can substantially contribute to the education of their child is critical to long-term success in engaging every family. While not a replacement for human engagement, technology and the growing interest in social media can play an important role in extending the efforts of school personnel to connect with all families.

With many schools and districts around the world harboring fear of the use of social media by teachers and administrators, the use of these tools by educators and parents in a positive and impactful way models for children the important notion of digital citizenship (DCit) or how we should be behaving online. Many districts have created reactive acceptable use policies (AUPs) that avoid social media tools to protect themselves as opposed to encouraging innovation. Schools and parents are in the best position to set the bar high with regard to creating not only lifelong learners but lifelong digital citizens.

MEETING PARENTS WHERE
THEY ARE: IN CYBERSPACE

Millions of people spend a portion of their day in the world of technology and social networking. Tech-savvy educators have figured out how to further enhance communicating and building relationships with families using technology and social media. A word of caution, however: As easy as social media has made it for all of us to connect, there is no substitute for face-to-face communication. Whenever possible, building relationships by speaking with people directly, eye-to-eye, is preferable.

With a strong belief in the value of family engagement, one can spend the time harnessing its power for school success as one of the pieces of the puzzle that supports the learning of all children. While on the surface a commitment to engagement is seemingly in conflict with using technology to stay connected with families, knowledge of core family engagement research and best practice ensure that all families can stay connected.

A first step into the world of technology and family engagement might be best served by determining the best way to communicate with families. Most of the time, asking and surveying parents for the best methods of communication is the quickest way to determine avenues. The use of Google mail and Google documents also allows more sharing of information when face-to-face conversations are not possible.

Google Hangouts

Google Hangouts is an instant messaging and video chat platform developed by Google. Google Hangouts is designed to be the future of social interaction in cyberspace.

Twitter

The most popular age group of today's Twitter user is 18 to 35, which is the age of current and future parents (Pew Research Center, 2015). Numerous schools are now using social media to connect with families by way of school Twitter and Facebook accounts. Offering training sessions for parents to become familiar with and use Twitter will increase its use. As more teachers and parents learn Twitter and adopt their own accounts, it opens up transparent opportunities for two-way communication while building the relationships needed to create true partnerships in the school.

Instagram

Instagram is an online mobile photo-sharing, video-sharing, and social networking service that enables its users to take pictures and videos and share them on a variety of social networking platforms, such as Facebook, Twitter, Tumblr, and Flickr.

The Real Revolution in Communication: Video

While there is plenty of research to show that social media has infiltrated just about every aspect of our lives, what may be growing more exponentially is the use of video. The use of video is so common in our everyday lives, we may not even know how much of an impact it truly has.

Video, according to Tiland (2014), has moved beyond entertainment to include business, politics, communication, and music. Presidential candidates are now using video to announce their candidacies. Video messaging is concise and easy to understand. And, video reaches everyone.

There is a huge application for video in family engagement. Consider for a moment the viral nature of the Kahn Academy. What started out as a few simple videos to help a relative with math turned into a worldwide phenomenon. From that we now have the concept of flipped classrooms—classrooms where the lesson is taught on video and the class time is used for practice and application. Why could we not do the same for families?

Consider making a one- to two-minute video that highlights your success with a family engagement strategy, and send it to our website, www .drsteveconstantino.com, for possible inclusion in our video library of engagement ideas.

Idea

Think of one or two things you could share with a parent or family member that would support the learning in your classroom this week. Then, make a short video and upload it to your teacher or school website.

PRINCIPLE #2: COMMUNICATE EFFECTIVELY AND BUILD RELATIONSHIPS

Description. There is consistent evidence that effective communication and relationship building creates environments in the schools that are welcoming, respectful, and conducive to family engagement. The school places an emphasis on effective communication with every family and stakeholder within the learning community and seeks to build trusting relationships with every family.

Where We Are

Based on the description, discuss and record where you think your school is today as it relates to the principle description.

(Continued)

(Continued)

2.1 The school creates and maintains a welcoming and respectful environment that is inviting, supportive, and encouraging to every family.

Best Practice Description

Families are surveyed annually to determine ways to maintain and improve the welcoming environment of the building. A standing committee is in place that continuously monitors and improves the welcoming environment of the school. Friendly and welcoming signs in multiple languages are posted at all intersections and points where families and guests must make a decision about direction.

The safety and security of all families and guests is evident, and accommodations for handicapped guests exist. The history and culture of the school are celebrated with artifacts on display. Through staff or volunteers, greeters welcome all families and guests, and translation is advertised and readily available. A family-oriented and family-operated program is in place to welcome and orient all new families to the school.

The school creates a comfortable area for families, such as a family resource center stocked with books, computers and Internet access, parenting tips, homework, and curricular information, and offers classes to families on a multitude of academic topics suggested by families and student achievement data. Student work adorns all offices and public areas of the school with explanations of standards and assessments and is rotated regularly. Pictures of students and staff adorn all areas, giving the school a sense of home and community. School events celebrate the culture of the community and are often cross-curricular in nature.

Relationships between teachers and family are evident by collaboration and encouragement from school staff to be engaged with the school and learning. Professional development is available to further improve interactions between families and teachers. Above all, school staff values the importance of building relationships with all families regardless of background. The school implements a process to garner continuous feedback on family engagement efforts.

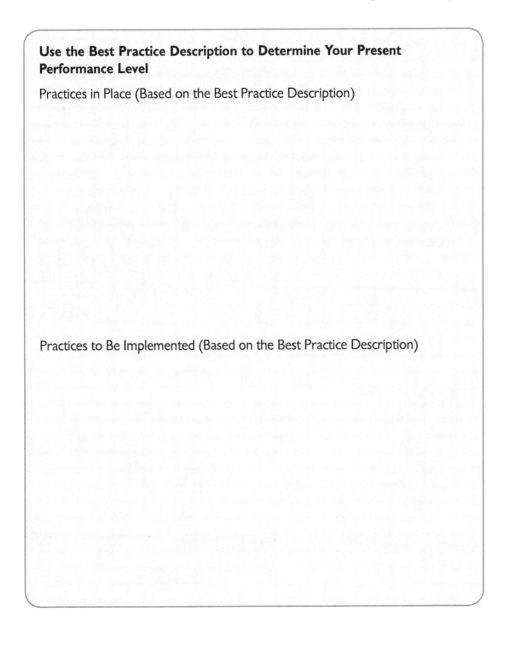

Use the Best Practice Description to Determine Your Present Performance Level

Practices in Place (Based on the Best Practice Description)

Practices to Be Implemented (Based on the Best Practice Description)

2.2 The school employs strategies that extend relationship-building opportunities beyond the school walls so that every family can substantially contribute to the education of their children.

Best Practice Description

The school moves beyond traditional satisfaction data to understand patterns of engagement. Data shows that families feel a sense of belonging to the school. All relationships with families are child centered. The school has developed a culture or belief statement(s) that supports the notion of building strong relationships with every family. Welcoming behaviors are consistent throughout the school staff.

Customer service goals are established and monitored. To garner a sense of caring, the school has multiple smaller gatherings for classrooms/ grade levels, and so forth, to make time between families and staff more meaningful and intimate. Families are recognized and embraced for their contributions however large or small, and the majority of families feel their efforts are acknowledged and validated.

School personnel accept all families at their station in life and do not hold expectations or build relationships with them based on school-driven ideas. Families feel comfortable expressing their ideas and concerns and are treated in a respectful manner, regardless of the circumstances.

All school staff are committed to home visitations, and the school regularly schedules meetings and events outside of the school, promoting a commitment to continuous outreach. Technology, including the extensive use of social media and other means, allows families access to staff and information, however, the commitment by the school for face-to-face inter-actions enhances family confidence in their child's school. Technology does not replace face-to-face contact and the important relationships that result.

Use the Best Practice Description to Determine Your Present Performance Level

Practices in Place (Based on the Best Practice Description)

Practices to Be Implemented (Based on the Best Practice Description)

2.3 The school ensures that healthy, two-way communication is consistently maintained. A sense of caring to truly collaborate with every family exists as evidenced by numerous mechanisms to allow families to communicate easily and directly with the school.

Best Practice Description

All staff in the school believe that two-way communication with all families is essential in the learning process. School staff create multiple avenues for two-way communication of learning goals and the ongoing assessment of those goals. Families are equally comfortable in contacting school staff about how they might better support learning goals at home.

Two-way communication is regular, and child-centered strategies for home learning and evidence of success are routinely shared. The school has a mechanism in place to allow teachers to regularly communicate with families for whom English is not a first language. All communication is easily understood and free of educational jargon. Families are routinely given examples and ideas of learning activities that can be accomplished at home that support standards being taught.

Families have timely access to current grades, assignments, standards, and other academic information that help them support their child(ren). Teachers publish calendars of activities far enough in advance to allow families time to plan. Teachers regularly use telephone, e-mail, texting, teacher web pages, and blogs to share information with families and communicate what is being taught in the classroom. Conferences are inclusive of students when appropriate, are scheduled at mutually convenient times, and focus on enhancing learning rather than deficit behaviors.

Conferences are student centered with the student participating. Home visits by all staff reinforce the school's commitment to families and learning and reinforces family confidence in their child's progress. The school solicits information on the best ways to communicate and uses that data to improve all forms of two-way communication. Families consistently report high satisfaction with the communication with their child's teacher, school, and school district. The school uses the feedback data to set new targets and improve systems.

Use the Best Practice Description to Determine Your Present Performance Level

Practices in Place (Based on the Best Practice Description)

Practices to Be Implemented (Based on the Best Practice Description)

NOTE

1. Strategies used with permission of Dr. Joni Samples, Family Friendly Schools.

7

Principle #3

Empower Every Family

Self-belief does not necessarily ensure success, but self-disbelief assuredly spawns failure.

—Albert Bandura

Families that believe they can make a positive difference in their children's educational lives are said to have a high level of "efficacy." Parental efficacy simply means that one possesses skills, abilities, and resources to parent effectively and improve the family's school and community or they are empowered to produce a positive effect on their child's educational outcomes. Empowered families see challenges as opportunities rather than roadblocks and hold high expectations for their children. They maintain a positive outlook on their child's ability to learn and be successful in school. Empowered families are more likely to be engaged with their children's educational experiences in a variety of ways, all of which support a healthy learning environment in school.

Principle #3: Empower Every Family

Description. Families are recognized as essential members of the learning team for each student—their participation is welcomed, valued, and encouraged by the school. The school understands that families are important and influential resources, because they know their children best.

3.1 The school makes a conscious effort to educate families to play a proactive role in the school life of their child throughout their school career.

3.2 Families participate in the development of the student's learning plan, help assess progress, and provide support for their child's learning.

3.3 Families suggest mentoring possibilities and use their local knowledge, personal skills, assets, and networks in ways that support the school's program.

3.4 The school has in place induction processes to welcome and support families who are new to the school.

CHANGING THE QUESTIONS: MY FAMOUS TEST

One of my absolute favorite portions of keynotes and workshops is when I ask the audience to take a simple test. It's a two-question test; miss one question and it will be immediate remediation with an expedited retake of the test. Thousands of people have taken the two-question test, and I am proud to report that no one has ever missed either of the questions.

I usually inform the audience that I will present a scenario and questions. When I point to the audience I ask them to shout out whatever answer comes to mind. It only works if everyone shouts the answer. No shyness allowed! So, let's see how you do with the famous test.

Here's the scenario: Somewhere in your school district this evening, a family finds themselves all at home, allowing an opportunity for the family to have dinner together—something that rarely happens. Mom is so thrilled to have her loved ones together that she skips the microwave and goes directly to the George Foreman . . . it's a special night!

While mom happily prepares dinner, dad decides he wants to have a conversation with his children about school. He gets their attention away from the distraction of cell phones, texting, Twitter, Instagram, Snapchat, or whatever application de jour keeps the children from conversing with their dad. When he is convinced he has their attention, he asks them this simple question. (Read the question and shout the answer out! Don't worry, no one will think you are crazy.)

What did you do in school today? (Answer: _____)

Undaunted by the first answer, dad goes in a second time with what he believes to be a logical follow-up question. (Read the question and shout the answer out.)

Do you have any homework? (Answer: _____)

If you answered "nothing" to question number one and "no" to question number two, congratulations, you aced the test. As audiences chuckle at the collective answers shouted by everyone, I like to give them something to think about.

Everyone answers those questions correctly, not because of my masterful teaching but because we (educators) have asked our own children the very same ones. All of us have. *All of us*. Given that the vast majority of audiences with which I have had the honor to work are tied to education in one form or fashion and clearly understand how to ask a better question, what hope then do families have who do *not* know what we as educators know? Answer? Not much. For some families, the elimination of hope is the last foundational support in believing their children will exceed them in their quality of life. This is a powerful emotion that drives family behaviors toward school.

Help families engage with their children about school on a meaningful and relevant level and you also accomplish these two things: You build efficacy, and you empower families to engage in the educational lives of their children. In other words, supply them with information that allows them to ask better questions. If we change the questions families ask, we have immediately empowered them to have a role in the education of their children. Empowerment is efficacy. Efficacy is empowerment. However, families cannot ask their children better questions if we do not assist them in understanding what happens in school everyday. Telling them what happened last week or last month isn't very helpful in promoting true empowerment.

What if a child walks through the door after school and a parent asks, "What is the order of operations?" or "Show me the quiz that you took in science today," or "Explain longitude and latitude to me." If we could figure out mechanisms to share this type of information with families, conversations between parents and children would change substantially and efficacy would take root. So how can we do it?

Here is what I know to be true: As educators we are really good at sending stuff home. We have mastered the art of one-way communication. As is highlighted in the section devoted to changing the weekly folder, sending home information about things that already have occurred will most likely not inspire a great deal of efficacy. However, sending things home that are interactive in nature, meaning they require a conversation between the student and their parent and some sort of response that will be returned to the teacher, will alter conversations and go a long way toward engaging every family regardless of who they are or their station in life.

Activity

Brainstorm with colleagues all the things you send home and all the ways you communicate with families about learning in school. Use the box below to record your ideas.

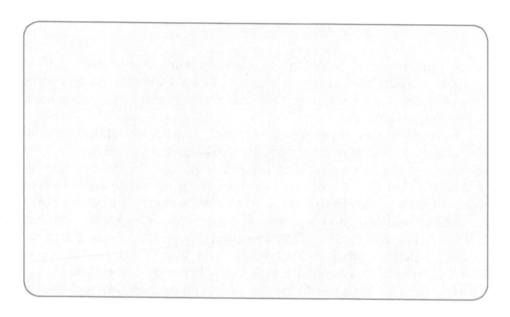

Now, think about ways you can take the information that you already send home and promote efficacy, by allowing parents to somehow engage with their children. Use the box below to record your ideas.

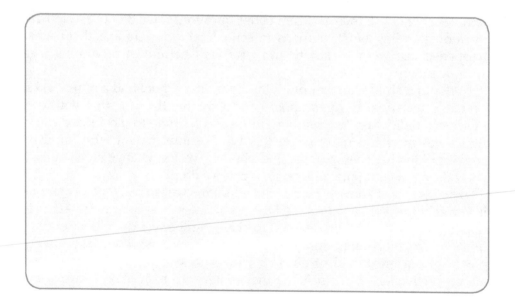

A GREAT IDEA TO CHANGE THOSE QUESTIONS

Twitter is a really powerful way to learn, gather information, share ideas, and meet (virtually) all types of educators from just about anywhere in the world. In just a few minutes, I find cutting-edge ideas, research, articles, blogs, and a host of other types of information. I can join chat groups created around topics of interest, and I can share my ideas and information with others. It is this venue where I found Jeromie Heath (@teachheath).

Let me be clear: I have never met Jeromie. I know that he is a teacher somewhere in the United States, and by visiting his website, I can narrow his location to a district in Washington State. I also know he is a National Board Certified Teacher, and after visiting his website, I can attest to his high level of engagement, creativity, and passion for teaching.

I was scrolling through tweets when I stumbled upon the following:

Try asking these questions to learn about your child's school experiences:

Parent – Student Questions

- **What new thing did you learn during [Reading/Math/Writing/Science] time today? How did you learn it?**

- **What is something that you learned today that you didn't know yesterday?**

- **What struggles did you have today and how did you overcome them?**

- **Why did you choose the book you are reading? Tell me your feelings about the story so far.**

- **What skill did you practice and learn in math today? How do you plan to get better?**

- **What is something you learned today that you think you will need in your future career?**

- **Teach me something. Pretend you are the teacher and I am you. Teach me something you learned today.**

@teachheath

Source: Used with permission of Jeromie Heath, @teachheath.

I loved this! This is a perfect example of how changing the conversation between children and families would support all of the good work that is being done in classrooms everyday and, equally important, would promote the efficacy of families. But I discovered that this information had been retweeted a number of times; finding the originator was going to be a challenge. To include this in the book, I needed to find the originator.

I noticed in the bottom corner of the question chart, there was a Twitter handle, @teachheath. This was going to be easier than I thought. I tweeted a message to Jeromie and within minutes, he tweeted back. Through this channel of communication, I received his permission to publish his question chart. Jeromie has a lot of great ideas; follow him on Twitter and Pinterest and check out his YouTube videos.

CREATING THE TRANSPARENT SCHOOL

A pioneer in family engagement research (and a great friend) is Dr. Jerold Bauch, Professor Emeritus at Vanderbilt University. I credit Jerry with exposing me to the whole notion of family engagement and setting me on the journey that I still travel today.

Jerry is a man who has always been ahead of his time. In 1989, he created "The Transparent School Model," a system by which computer-assisted telephone technology could be used to connect parents and teachers every day to support the home learning of students (Bauch, 1989). It's important to remember that in 1989 there was no Internet or cell phones, no Twitter, Snapchat, Instagram, Voxer, or Facebook. We had a telephone. (At least it had buttons instead of a rotary dial.)

Ninety percent of American adults have a cell phone, with 58% of adults having a smart phone (Pew Research Center, 2015). Interestingly, 67% of us check our cell phones for calls, texts, and alerts even if they are not ringing or vibrating! Consider for a moment the sheer magnitude of differences in communication between 1989 and 2015.

Take the seemingly antiquated technology of the home phone and 1980s voicemail out of the equation and focus on the concept: a method using technology that allowed for robust two-way communication between teachers and families, every day if they wished, about school activities so that parents could have a more meaningful conversation with their children and ask them better questions. In those days, teachers would take a simple voicemail system and, instead of parents leaving messages for teachers to contact them, teachers would leave messages, less than a minute long, about what happened in school (or class at the high school level). Read the following paragraph and time yourself. How long does it take you to read it?

Hello. My name is Tom Smith, and today is January 1, 2015. I am your child's third period algebra teacher. All this week we will be studying the order of operations, multiplication, division, addition, and subtraction. It is important that your child understand the order of operations, because all of our work in algebra is built on this important concept. What you could do for me this week is ask your child to share the order of operations and make sure they say multiplication, division, addition, and subtraction. You can remember the order yourself by saying the phrase My Dear Aunt Sally. We are having a quiz on this information on Friday, so attendance this week is very important. When you call again next Monday, I will tell you how the quiz went and the next exciting thing we are doing in algebra. And, as always, if there is anything I need to know about your child, please press the pound sign and leave me a message.

How long did it take you to read that passage? (It took me 43 seconds.) If you are an average reader, it should have taken you under a minute. By leaving this message, you have shared specific information with parents about how they can interact with their children about school in a much better manner, and you have increased support for home learning, which translates into better class participation and grades. You have promoted the efficacy of parents in the educational lives of their children, and you have given families a meaningful process by which to establish a two-way communication and better relationships. And, it took you a minute!

Here's the question to ask yourself:

Is less than a minute of my time worth better student achievement for every child?

Today's technology has far surpassed the 1989 telephone, but the concept of *The Transparent School Model* is as relevant today as it was when conceived by Dr. Bauch in 1989. Let's see how we might apply these ideas to today's technology.

Activity

You have learned the basic premise of the Transparent School Model: Use technology to promote parent efficacy and home learning by sharing information about school on a daily or regular basis. Apply this concept to the following modern-day technology applications. How could you re-create the Transparent School Model using

Facebook?

Twitter?

(Continued)

(Continued)

Instagram?

Pinterest?

Web pages?

Cell phones?

E-mail?

Texts?

Other technology available to you?

CASE STUDY: CLASS ISN'T THE SAME WITHOUT YOU

Jessica Mulhaney teaches geometry at the local high school. Jessica is a very popular teacher and there are always more students and families requesting Jessica as a teacher than can be accommodated by the school. She is friendly and supportive of students, builds strong relationships with families, and simultaneously holds high standards in place for all of her students. She has the highest pass rate on the state geometry test of all the teachers in her school district.

Several years ago, Jessica went through the Transparent School Model Training. She immediately saw applications for her classroom and began to use the voicemail system as taught in the professional development class. As part of that training and process implementation, Jessica encourages families to leave her messages about what is happening outside of school that could cause an interference with learning. She learned long ago that teenagers' emotions run the gamut and when behaviors are odd there is usually something provoking them.

On a very typical Thursday morning, her first-period geometry students began to wander into the classroom—some energetic, some still wiping cobwebs from their eyes. A few students were downing their last sips of coffee and soda as well as the last

(Continued)

(Continued)

bites of their mobile breakfasts. Suddenly, Jason entered the room in a manner she had never seen before. He threw his book bag to the floor and himself onto his desk. He immediately covered his head with his arms. When a classmate asked what was wrong, Jason became angry and yelled for the classmate to mind their own business. Another classmate, feeling Jason was unreasonable, scolded him for his behavior. This action made Jason even more angry. He jumped from his seat and postured as if he was going to fight the other student.

Jessica tried to intervene and Jason ignored her. Once again, he angrily sat down, covered his head with his arms, and told Jessica to "get lost." Under normal circumstances, Jason most likely would have been removed from class and sent to the assistant principal's office for discipline. But, Jessica didn't take that action. She knew something and that something changed the course of her interaction with Jason.

Upon her arrival to school that morning, Jessica listened to her messages. There was one message, and it was from Jason's mother. She explained that the family had been through a traumatic ordeal the evening before; the beloved family dog passed away. Jason's mother went on to explain that the dog had been there since Jason was a small child and that he and his sister were taking the death of the dog quite hard. Jason didn't sleep at all during the night. His mother ended the message by saying "If he is not doing well, please let me know. I am happy to come and get him. I told him not to go to school today, but he insisted he had to go."

Jessica calmly walked over to Jason, whose head was still down buried under his arms. She spoke in a whisper:

"Jason, I am very sorry about what happened to your dog. I cannot imagine how you must feel today. Please know that I truly do understand." Jason didn't move.

"I am not going to bother you today. However, if and when you are ready and you want to participate, I welcome your involvement. You know, Jason, class is never the same without you." With that, Jessica left Jason and started class.

About fifteen minutes into class, Jason raised his head, opened his book, and joined the class.

Questions for Discussion

1. What do you think would have occurred if Jessica did not have the opportunity to listen to the message Jason's mother left?

2. What actions did Jessica take that made this situation work out the way it did?

3. How did Jessica's action promote efficacy and trust in the relationships between herself, the student, and the parent?

4. Has something similar ever happened to you as a teacher? If so, how did you handle the situation?

5. What can we learn from this case study that we can apply to real-world situations?

SO, SIMPLY PUT, WHAT IS EFFICACY?

The idea of self-efficacy is simple: It refers to the belief that one has the ability or capability to act in ways that will produce whatever outcomes are desired (Bandura, 1997). One can argue that it is human nature to consider potential outcomes of an action before one decides to take the action. The same holds true for family engagement and efficacy. In other words, if we don't see our engagement with something producing any desirable or different results, the likelihood of our engagement is significantly diminished. The key to effective engagement is to make experiences for families both meaningful and relevant to them. *Meaningful* and *relevant* are two very important words when engaging every family.

I can hear your argument: *We offer a lot of things for parents, but they simply don't show up.* We have already learned that there are many challenges facing families that either limit their engagement or that have created circumstances for them to be disengaged. Sending a flyer home about an important meeting may or may not resonate with a family. They may not understand how this meeting is relevant to them or their children. But when we take a different approach and personalize activities and explain how the activity will positively impact their child or why this activity is essential to their child's development, we have promoted their efficacy and, over time, their attendance or participation will improve.

Efficacy is not about possessing specific skills or knowledge. For example, family engagement with homework in secondary schools tends to wane largely because the parent or family member does not believe they possess the knowledge to assist their child. Efficacy is focused on how the family member approaches a problem or task and accesses needed support, not what knowledge they possess.

An empowered parent, for example, is more likely to participate in a workshop so she can help her child with math homework or language skills. The same parent may take a series of classes on understanding the Internet or how to help children find resources on the Internet. Efficacy provides a parent the belief that her involvement makes a difference to her child and the ultimate learning outcomes of that child. If she doesn't know something or some way to help her child, she will seek out what she needs from the school or some other community service.

Families make decisions about their involvement and engagement in part by thinking about the potential outcomes of that involvement (Hoover-Dempsy, Walker, & Sandler, 2005). I'm sure all of us can think of an experience that encapsulates the idea stated above. Family members who believe they can make a difference in their children's lives, including their learning life, are important resources for schools. They cannot make a difference if we do not assist them in seeing the value.

Many families do not participate in parent-teacher conferences in secondary schools, sometimes because they believe that their involvement in them will produce no beneficial or desirable outcome or, more commonly, that their child is "old enough" to work through school issues by themselves. Almost every family has period of struggle in the educational lives of their children. Consider this dialog taken from a conference between a teacher and parents of a ninth-grade student:

Counselor: *Your son could be doing better in school.*

Parents: *We understand.*

Counselor: *He could do better if he applied himself. He has great potential.*

Parents: *We believe he has potential too. He did so well in the lower grades.*

Counselor: *If he completed his homework, his grades would be better.*

Parents: *We are never sure what homework he has. He says he never has any.*

As difficult as it may be, we must ask ourselves: If we were a parent in an hourly wage job (meaning if we take time off, we do not get paid) would we find the conversation that is referenced above meaningful enough to repeat again?

If conferences do not address the questions and issues that parents have for their children's education, then they are no longer meaningful or relevant. The all-too-familiar exchange above could be significantly altered if, prior to the conference, the parents were asked what they wanted to glean from the meeting. Given that most parents have the capability to monitor attendance and grades on the Internet without creating meaningful dialog, there is no incentive for parents to attend. Seeing no real opportunity for empowerment, the participation stops. It shouldn't be surprising to us.

Try This

The next time there is a conference scheduled, reach out to the family by phone or in person and use the following dialog: *We are very happy to have the opportunity to talk with you about (student's) progress in school. As we prepare, what questions do you have? What would you like to know as a result of our conference? How can we make this a meaningful experience for you?*

In its simplest definition, efficacy can be described as empowering someone to have an effect on something. In the case of family efficacy, it is the families' power to affect their children's education. There is much attention paid to teacher and student efficacy, with a great deal of literature devoted to the ideas that promoting both brings about more success in student learning and performance. Most schools and districts would not hesitate to promote the ideas of efficacy for teachers and students through professional learning and growth opportunities.

In contrast, there is much less attention and discussion paid to the idea of promoting family efficacy as a conduit to improved student achievement. The sense of efficacy for helping children succeed in school is an important contributor to how and why parents decided to be involved and engaged with their children's learning (Hoover-Dempsey, Walker, and Sandler, 2005).

Hoover-Dempsey and Sandler (1997) are influential researchers in the area of family efficacy. They found that parents' sense of efficacy, meaning their view of their own ability to help their children with school-related work, primarily focused on the extent that parents believed that through their engagement they could exert positive influence on the children's educational outcomes. Parents clearly make choices as to the level of their involvement with their child's education. Those choices are often directly connected to their own perceptions of their ability to help their child.

A major factor in parents making positive decisions with regard to their role in education is determined by their perception of a parental role in general or, more specifically, what they believe they should and should not be doing as parents (Hoover-Dempsey and Sandler, 1997). Roles in any organization inclusive of parents and school personnel are characterized by the interaction between the members of the group over time.

Thus, if school personnel interact with every family, then every family would understand that supporting and extending learning was a basic function of the parental role. Conclusively, school personnel can shape the role parents and families perceive they should play with regard to engagement in school-related activities and the academic lives of their own children. Schools that discourage, limit, or simply place little value on engaging families are helping to shape parental role perception that will continue to plague the culture of the school.

Empowering every family, then, is the notion that parents and families can help to produce positive educational outcomes with their child. Traditional avenues of parent involvement do not take into consideration building the capacity—the efficacy—of parents to transfer knowledge from school to their children.

Generally speaking, practices that promote parental efficacy

1. Are grounded in student achievement and parent perceptional data

2. Are action oriented, meaning parents learn by doing, then transfer the knowledge to their children

3. Take parental levels of education into consideration

4. Work around barriers to successful family engagement

5. Meet parent and family needs

6. Are part of a larger process to promote family engagement

> **Quick Tip: Designing Opportunities for Families**
>
> Most teachers design workshops and other experiences for parents and families to better help them understand student-learning expectations. More often than not, however, teachers design these events. The contents of the events are decided upon and controlled by teachers. To help the experience be more meaningful and relevant to families, solicit their input on their needs. Ask them what they need to know or want to know. Design opportunities based on family feedback. Attendance will start to climb, and support will start to improve!

Anne Stilwell and Dianne Ferguson (n.d.) published a report that shares four ways for schools to assist families to increase their sense of efficacy and that is reprinted here with permission.

> **Promote successful personal experiences for family members.** Anytime family members feel welcome and effective in school when talking with school personnel or when working with their children, they are developing belief in their ability to make a difference. Schools that have volunteers who greet families, help them feel comfortable, and accomplish their reasons for coming to school create a successful experience.
>
> Teachers who ask and listen to families—trying to understand their values and preferences in order to tailor learning and curriculum for students—help family members feel like they are an important part of schooling. Building positive associations with parent involvement helps enhance the parent's sense of efficacy—he believes his participation has a positive impact on his child's learning—and increases the likelihood of continued future involvement.
>
> **Help family members learn from each other.** Helping family members have successful experiences can also be indirect. When school personnel connect families that might have experiences to share, they expand feelings of success. Hearing about other students' experiences, learning from teachers who are successful with students, sharing with other families in similar and different family situations all build confidence, knowledge, and efficacy.
>
> Teachers could model efficacious behavior to parents ("When I run across something I don't know, this is how I search for the answer.") or design workshops where parents can witness good responses to various situations.
>
> **Always offer encouragement.** School personnel don't always agree with families' choices or perspectives. Sometimes these differences are fleeting and easily resolved with more complete communication. Sometimes the differences are deeper reflections of culture, values, and history. Nevertheless, school professionals are in positions of power with respect to many families. Many parents feel that teachers' opinions and ideas hold more weight then their own. Families' ideas and feelings can easily be crushed by a busy teacher, and their feelings of efficacy diminished.

A good solution is for school personnel to always take an encouraging stance with family members, even when they don't completely understand their position or might even disagree. Encouragement coming from someone with more currency and power can ensure ongoing communication instead of inadvertently shutting it down. After a parent volunteers on a project, sending a thank-you note that comments on a job well done helps her feel that her contribution makes a difference. Persuasion is another way of offering encouragement. Persuading the parent that her involvement is appreciated and has a positive effect increases her sense of efficacy.

Focus on emotional well-being and stress reduction. Stress poses a big threat to parental efficacy. Anything the school can do to foster calm and reduce tension will help increase families' ability to make a difference This might mean providing specific tools or community resources to parents so that they can feel more in control of their lives. If lack of food is stressing a family out, hook them up with food banks. If it's lack of health care that's the problem, brainstorm options with the family and make referrals. Sometimes the act of listening itself can help reduce stress.

DO WE NEED TO INTERACT WITH EVERY FAMILY?

The question posed above may seem antithetical to the whole premise of this book. The question, however, is an important one and may hold the key to unlocking more potential to promoting family efficacy and improving learning outcomes for all children.

Family social class also plays a role in the degree to which families believe in their own efficacy with their children's education. Social class influences parent decision making in shaping home support roles (Lareau, 1987). Many parents and families that are deemed socioeconomically disadvantaged suffer the additional burdens of having less education and low income. They view their own abilities as significantly lower than that of the economically advantaged counterparts and as such often send their children to school and simply hope for the best (Eccles & Harold, 1994).

Consider, for a moment, the desire to host math night for all parents in a particular grade level or subject. An evening meeting dedicated to assisting families usually begins with planning. Teachers plan a meeting that includes information and possibly activities to help families understand what their children are learning in school. A great deal of effort goes into designing a meeting that is both informative and engaging.

A letter is usually sent to all of the families announcing the special meeting and encouraging all families to attend. The letter is usually sent home with students or sometimes attached to the weekly newsletter published by the school or a parent organization. Either way, time, energy, resources, and talent are invested in communicating this important evening. Teachers and school staff usually arrange for light snacks and in some cases, babysitting services for younger children, understanding that the only way families can attend is to bring children along.

Generally speaking, when the meeting night arrives one of two scenarios emerge. The first scenario includes more teachers present than parents. The second scenario seems on the surface a bit more successful: a full complement of parents and family members eager to learn. Upon closer examination the full room of parents are usually those parents of students who are thoroughly engaged with school and whose children are usually successful: This is often described as *engaging the already engaged.* Parents who attend have usually garnered significant self-efficacy and are engaged with the school and their children's education at many levels. I often ask teachers in workshops, "If you have a roomful of parents, are they the parents who needed to be there?" The answer is almost always "no."

Schools that wish to engage those that are traditionally non-engaged or less engaged understand that at the core is the use of student data that targets and focuses on a subset of families whose children could benefit from their understanding of and engagement with schoolwork.

More importantly, the notion of learning at home seems to be a more stringent predictor in family engagement practices that supports student learning. Whether at home or at school, motivating parents and families to become engaged is the key first step to promoting better success for every student and family.

WHAT MOTIVATES PARENTS?

The Hoover-Dempsey, Walker, and Sandler model (2005) includes three motivational sources of parental engagement with learning. The first centers on parents' motivational beliefs that include the construction of the role of the parent and parental beliefs about their self-efficacy to support their children while in school.

The second is the degree to which parents and families believe that the school values their participation and the genuine nature of the invitation to become engaged, and the third is the contexts of parent personal lives and how those inform their own perception of whether or not it is feasible for them to be engaged and the degree to which they believe their own skill, time, and energy is conducive to their engagement.

The salient question for discussion is this: Do families really believe that through their efforts to become engaged in the school-learning lives of their children that they can exercise a more positive outcome in their children's school performance? Families will set preconceived goals for their involvement with school. These goals run along a continuum of low to high and are directly related to a parent's belief in their own efficacy (Hoover-Dempsey & Sandler, 1997). It stands to reason then that schools would be well served to interact with families and support parent and family knowledge. By doing so, families' views of their own efficacy will rise and, ultimately, so will their engagement with their child.

INTERACTIVE HOMEWORK DESIGN

An excellent idea for promoting the efficacy of families is to design homework assignments that engage families or interact with them. Rather than families who simply ask, "Did you do your homework?" families can have a role in the homework and lesson. With the advent of the use of technology and flipped classrooms, there are even more opportunities to engage families outside of the school.

We often consider family engagement as activities that happen at school, activities that we can see. Consider for a moment that promoting the efficacy of families relies on those types of activities that we inspire but may not see. It is more likely that these types of activities will happen in the home and not at school. While we don't see the actual engagement, we can clearly see the results of that engagement. I refer to this as *invisible engagement*: engagement we don't necessarily see but of which we see the results.

The National Network of Partnership Schools (NNPS) promotes an excellent interactive homework design project called TIPS: Teachers Involve Parents in Schoolwork (Epstein, Salinas, & Jackson, 1995). The TIPS philosophy requires students to talk to someone at home about something interesting that they are working on in class. Parents are not responsible to teach the student the information and, many times, it's the other way around, with children teaching their parents. Teaching another person what you have learned is an excellent way to ensure that learning has taken place!

Check out the National Network of Partnership Schools website for more information on the TIPS program.

http://www.csos.jhu.edu/tips/OVERVIEW.htm

STUDENT-LED CONFERENCES

Consider the following statement:

Human beings will make time for whatever they deem important to them.

This statement has a resounding impact for all of us. The next time you ask someone to do something and they decline citing time as the reason, you might now wonder if it truly is time or level of importance.

To engage families and to build their efficacy, we need to create opportunities for them that provide information that is meaningful and relevant. Their lives are busy and complicated. Sending a flyer home and indicating that the annual conferences are coming up will solicit responses from the "already engaged" families. To improve the attendance of families who are traditionally disengaged or for whatever reasons do not attend conferences and meetings, consider a student-led model. When students are part of the equation, the experience instantly becomes much more meaningful and relevant to families.

The idea of student-led conferences has been around for a while but continues to grow in popularity, especially at the secondary level. Individual student-led conferences at the high school level, for example, are far more productive in helping families understand the successes and challenges their own children face and are more likely to build the efficacy necessary to support improved achievement.

SHARING DATA WITH FAMILIES

It is nearly impossible to have a thorough discussion of promoting family efficacy without including the ideas of data sharing. With data driving everything from daily instruction to school district evaluation, it is imperative that we learn how to share appropriate and relevant data with families. There are great benefits to student learning when families understand data and what they can do to promote better learning at home.

Approaching data sharing with families is best done in the context of the whole child. Families need reassurances in our high-stakes testing environment that their children's future does not depend on one test score or that we make evaluations on student progress through multiple measures, such as attendance, classroom observations, and so forth (Harvard Family Research Project, 2013).

Teachers can work together to determine how to present data to families. In some cases, it is important to remember cultural backgrounds and communication protocols for different cultures. Finding appropriate ways of communicating data (privacy), sharing a range of data to show the whole child, and giving families a voice in the conversation all lead to better family understanding of student progress (Harvard Family Research Project, 2013).

Lastly, teachers are best served to avoid the use of jargon and acronyms, focus data conversations on areas of growth and improvement that can be supported by families, and provide families with potential resources that can be used with children outside of school (Harvard Family Research Project, 2013).

What Ideas Do You Have?

Promoting efficacy among families is allowing families to have a hand in the education of their children. It does not transfer the responsibility solely to families, but allows them to be part of the equation in a way that is meaningful and relevant to them. Some ideas have already been presented in this chapter. Considering what you have learned about promoting family efficacy, what additional ideas do you have? Jot them down here and come back later to work on an implementation plan.

CASE STUDY: TRYING TO TALK TO THE MATH TEACHER

Mr. and Mrs. Jones were very engaged in their children's education. Their older daughter seemed to sail through school effortlessly, but their middle son, Bobby, struggled. Bobby always ended up passing classes, but the Joneses were always concerned that he was teetering on the edge of academic disaster and feared what would occur as he transitioned to middle school and high school.

It was during his eighth-grade year that the Joneses' fears started to materialize. They received an interim report card indicting that Bobby was failing Algebra I. Not wanting too much time to go by, Mr. Jones contacted Bobby's guidance counselor to set up a meeting with the math teacher. The Joneses were interested in what more they could do at home to increase Bobby's success in math.

The guidance counselor was very pleasant with Mr. Jones and empathized with his concern. She also commended Mr. Jones for being proactive and asking for the meeting. Mr. Jones told the counselor that he realized the teachers were busy and he would change his schedule, regardless of what he had to do, to accommodate the

(Continued)

(Continued)

math teacher's schedule and needs. The counselor indicated that the best time for the teacher was 12:30 p.m. They set a date.

"So let me confirm what we said," started Mr. Jones. "My wife and I will be meeting with the math teacher on Thursday at 12:30 p.m., correct?"

"Oh, Mr. Jones, the meeting will be with the entire team, not just the math teacher," responded the counselor. Until this point, there had been no mention that the meeting would include Bobby's other teachers.

"I must not have been clear, I apologize," said Mr. Jones. "We really only need to talk with the math teacher. He seems to be doing pretty well everywhere else."

"Mr. Jones, our policy is that when a parent requests a meeting with a teacher, the entire team comes to the meeting. That is the way we do it here."

"I don't really need to waste the time of the other teachers," Mr. Jones said as he started to get agitated with the conversation. "We are really wanting to focus on math."

"I realize what you want to focus on, Mr. Jones. But the teachers are the experts, and they can tell you what to focus on. The other team members may have suggestions for you and your wife." The counselor sensed Mr. Jones was becoming irritated.

"Look," snapped Mr. Jones, "I don't want to meet with the other teachers, and I don't need to meet with the other teachers. I simply want a meeting with my son's math teacher. Are you going to set that up or not?"

"Mr. Jones, there is no need to become cross with me . . ."

Mr. Jones cut her off. "Lady, listen. I don't know what kind of policies you have at that school, but I think I have the right to meet with whomever I want to meet with, and in this instance, I want to meet with the math teacher." Mr. Jones was now angry.

"Mr. Jones, here is what you need to understand. If you want to have a meeting on Thursday at 12:30 p.m. to talk about your son's math problems, you will meet with the entire team or there will be no meeting. I'm sorry you disagree with our practice, but we find that it is quite effective in dealing with our youngsters and their parents." The counselor was firm and final in her tone.

"Fine," yelled Mr. Jones. "I'll meet with the whole darn team just to talk to one person. I've never heard of anything so stupid in all my life." With that he slammed down the phone.

At the meeting, the five teachers on the team sat in a row behind student desks. Two chairs with no desks were set up in front of the teachers. The assistant principal, who was not scheduled to be there, arrived to the meeting and began it. The Joneses had no idea that the assistant principal would be present at the meeting.

"Mr. Jones, I know you are upset with the school, and your tone with the guidance counselor was uncalled for. I think your anger is a bit displaced. We are here to talk about your son and his failure to comply with his teacher's requirements, which are now resulting in his failure. I am quite sure we can have a meeting today that is professional and calm. If not, then I will end the meeting abruptly, and it will continue with just me in my office. Is that understood?"

The meeting was scheduled to last twenty minutes. Each teacher took three to five minutes to share information about Bobby's grades, assignments, tests, and abilities. The math teacher reported that Bobby did not do his homework, and if he applied himself, he would do better in math. The Joneses never asked a question and never spoke a word.

The Joneses left the meeting and withdrew Bobby from the school that day.

Questions for Discussion

1. What are your thoughts about the policy of meeting the entire team of teachers when a conference with one is requested?

2. How did the policy promote family efficacy? Why?

3. Why do you think the team meeting philosophy is in place at this school?

4. How could this conference have provided a better outcome for all involved?

CASE STUDY: TEACHING RESPONSIBILITY?

David Smith was a high school senior and was facing a comprehensive test in math. If David failed the test, he would not be allowed to graduate. David had failed the test one time before. David's parents noticed that he seemed very stressed and withdrawn. Usually talkative, David was now quiet, choosing to sit in his room rather than be with the rest of his family and the family dog, whom David had loved since getting him as a puppy in fifth grade.

" I'm going to fail again, I just know it," yelled David when his mother tried to talk with him about his sullen mood.

"Maybe I can talk with your teacher. She might be able to help me understand what we can do to get you through this test. You know, I was pretty good in math in my day," David's mother said lovingly.

"Do what you want, Mom, it won't make any difference. I am not going to graduate with my friends because of this stupid test. Let's just face it." David stormed away from his mother.

The following day, David's mother made an appointment to see the teacher. David's two older siblings had had the same teacher for math, so she felt as though she knew the teacher and had a rapport that might help her better understand how to help her son.

"Thank you for meeting with me on such short notice," said Mrs. Smith.

"No problem at all," responded the math teacher. "I am happy to answer any questions you might have."

"As you probably know, David is frantic over this math test and feels defeated. He is already predicting he will fail and that he will not graduate with his class. This test is the only thing that is standing in his way. I thought perhaps you could give me some materials or guidance as to how my husband and I might help David at home. He still has a week before the test. If I knew what areas he was weak in, we could work with him."

"Mrs. Smith," began the teacher, "I applaud you for wanting to help your son, I really do. But he is seventeen years old. Don't you think it's time that he took responsibility for himself? His parents won't always be there to bail him out of trouble."

"We are not looking to bail David out of trouble. We were hoping that there were some problems or worksheets or other materials that you could point us to so that we could work with him at home to prepare for the test. If we knew what areas he was struggling with, we could emphasize that." Mrs. Smith's tone remained calm and reasonable.

"David has been given everything he needs to be successful on that test. I do not have the time to create individual support packets for every student who decides now, in their senior year, to take their education seriously. You should be asking David for this information, not me. At some point, we need to teach our young people to take responsibility. I teach responsibility to my students. It is my job. It is not my job to ensure that every student passes the test. I provide the materials to the students. I show them how to solve the problems. The rest is up to them. They have to have some skin in the game."

The math teacher agreed to give Mrs. Smith the same study packet that she had given to David. She also mentioned that the study packet was to have been completed and turned in for a grade. David did not turn his in and received two zeros, since the assignment was given double weight. He failed the course as a result.

David did not pass the comprehensive test and did not graduate. He chose not to attend summer school and got a job at the local supermarket instead.

Questions for Discussion

1. Was the request of David's mother reasonable? Why or why not?

2. What are your thoughts on the teacher's handling of this conference?

3. How did this exchange improve or impede family efficacy?

4. How could this situation be altered to improve the likelihood of family efficacy?

Quick Tip: Confronting the "We Already Tried That" Syndrome

Honestly, there may not be very many strategies left to engage families that haven't been conceived and tried by educators. Unfortunately, more often than not, the ideas were quickly abandoned when they did not provide the expected outcomes. Later, when the idea is revived, a chorus of "we tried that already and it didn't work" rises up to meet the new (old) idea. In most cases, the strategies were good ones. The reason for their failure or poor outcomes had little to do with the strategy and more to do with the lack of developing empowering practices for success. List those things that you have already tried and then apply the concepts of family efficacy to them. You will see, when you try them again, an improved outcome!

Things We Have Tried	Looking Through a New Lens of Efficacy: What Can We Do Differently?

(Continued)

(Continued)

Questions to Ponder

1. How often do you provide families information about their children's academic progress?

2. How do you encourage family involvement with creating enhanced home learning environments and activities?

3. Are your school planning and curriculum documents available to families?

4. Does your school require conferences with all families of students?

Available for download at www.drsteveconstantino.com

A CRITICAL COMPONENT OF INVITING FAMILY PARTICIPATION

So far, we know that to engage families in the learning lives of their children we must change our approach. We don't have to add more time or spend more money to do so, we simply need to look at our present practice and modify it based on the Five Simple Principles. Let's take a look at a common practice and how to improve it so that more families are engaged.

This entire chapter is about promoting the efficacy of parents, empowering them to have a positive effect on the education and learning of their children. We spend a great deal of time creating experiences for parents to participate in meetings, events, and workshops designed to help them support their children and understand better what is being learned in school and why. Educators spend a great deal of time encouraging families to participate. Over and over, we stress the importance of their engagement and involvement with whatever it is we deem valuable.

We encourage, demand, and even at times guilt parents into participation in these events. Even then, there are still parents who, for reasons we have learned, do not participate. After planning and executing the event, what is it we then do with those parents who did not attend? The answer: Nothing. Usually, we shrug our shoulders, assume they don't care, and move on.

Consider this: If someone repeatedly told you that taking a specific action was important to your well-being, hammering the idea that the action is absolutely necessary and essential, then said nothing more to you after you didn't take the action, what would you think? The logical conclusion is that the action must not have been that important. This is exactly the idea we reinforce in parents who do not participate in the events we plan. We do nothing and reinforce to them that it wasn't important after all.

There is a simple remedy to this. For each of the parents that do not participate, call them immediately and say, "I am sorry that you could not participate (nonjudgmental) in our event. I still think this information is important. How can I get it to you?" This simple communication can alter the course of family engagement and efficacy in the child's education by communicating the importance of the parents' participation. Do this a few times and watch the changes occur.

BUILDING SUCCESSFUL RELATIONSHIPS WITH EVERY FAMILY: TEN PRACTICAL APPLICATIONS FOR CLASSROOM TEACHERS

Any teacher can incorporate family engagement principles so that children's classroom learning engages families and provides the home-learning support that teachers are desperate to attain. The following ten practices are designed to help every teacher build better relationships with all families, with an emphasis on building relationships with those families that are disengaged from their child's learning.

1. Relationships are the key.

Disengaged families have lost trust in the educational system. Many families who create disingenuous relationships with teachers do so because of past experiences. Every teacher has a wonderful opportunity to rekindle a strong and healthy relationship with all families, which is the first step in rebuilding trust:

- Make your first contact with families a positive one, with no agenda except to say hello and begin a dialog.
- Use language that families can understand. Many disengaged families may have weak educational capital and are reluctant to get into dialogs with teachers.
- Ask parents to share their concerns and opinions about school and then address those concerns.
- Work within your professional learning community to accommodate parents' work schedules.

2. Make learning meaningful and relevant.

Making learning meaningful and relevant to parents and families means providing families with information on current and upcoming classroom activities so that parents and families can ask their children better questions. When learning becomes more meaningful and relevant to parents and families, they are more engaged in supporting learning outcomes at home. Provide specific information to parents so that the questions they ask contain the attributes of the ones below:

- Tell me about (the order of operations, the book report draft that is due tomorrow, etc.)

- Show me (the story you have to read tonight, the book chapter that you are going to be tested on this Friday, etc.)
- Teach me (multiplication tables, Spanish, etc.)

3. Communicate what is coming, not what has passed.

Teachers spend a significant amount of time trying to communicate with families only to feel frustrated at the relatively low response levels from the homes of their students. In many cases, the communication from schools, such as grade reports or weekly folders, communicate what has already taken place.

Change the premise of communication to upcoming learning instead of learning that has passed. Send a weekly folder home that contains information about what is going to happen in class over the next week as opposed to what has already happened. Many teachers use a variety of apps to share information with parents and families about what occurred in school today and what will occur tomorrow. Consistently communicating upcoming learning will begin to engage more families, because learning is now meaningful and relevant to families and they now have information so that they can support classroom learning at home.

4. Share hopes and concerns and make a plan.

Parents and families desire the opportunity to dialog about the hopes and dreams they have for their children. All families, regardless of their ethnicity or socioeconomic status, want what is best for their children so that each child can prosper and exceed them in quality of life (Constantino, 2003).

Teachers should seek avenues to have these types of discussions with the parents and families of their children. To enhance the traditional parent conference, take some time to understand the hopes and dreams of families. Listen to their concerns and fears about their children. Practices that honor the contributions of families help strengthen relationships (Mapp, 2003). Use the commonality of the desire of success to create goals and plans with parents and families that not only help children achieve at higher levels but send a clear and powerful message to families that teachers do care a great deal.

5. Link communication to learning.

Many schools instinctively believe that the school newsletter is read by very few parents and families. Understanding that the goal in engaging families is to make their child's learning meaningful and relevant, how we communicate learning goals with families becomes a centerpiece of engaging them in the educational lives of their children.

Classroom newsletters that are short (one page) and more frequent (weekly) are read more often by more parents than a longer monthly newsletter that is distributed by the school. Whether sent home in a book-bag or posted online, newsletters are meaningful and relevant to families, because they are linked to their own child's learning. The classroom news-letter can be linked to learning in class *that week*. For example, share the state standard that is being met by the lessons that week. Choose one or two subject areas.

Share what is being taught and provide families an activity that can be done at home or provide information that families can ask their children to reinforce learning. For example, at the bottom of the weekly classroom newsletter, the teacher may write: *Ask your child about dinosaurs. Write down what they tell you and send this back to class tomorrow.* If there is a television program to be broadcast that will enhance learning that week, remind families of the program. Most importantly, provide an area for families to feed back information to you. Ask them to share their experiences or record the results of an activity. The engagement of families and students will begin to improve when communication is linked to learning.

In many of today's classrooms, the classroom newsletter has morphed into texts and tweets. However information is shared, it should inspire family empowerment in learning outside of the school.

6. Use a classroom website/social media/other technology.

The use of teacher and classroom websites as well as apps and social media has increased in popularity. Keep in mind the following informa-tion when working with technology:

- Determine the percentage of families that have access to the Internet. If everyone does not have access, posting information to the web alone will not engage all families.
- Be current and consistent with information. The greatest detriment to classroom websites and other technology is the failure to keep information current. Families who visit and find old or outdated information do not visit again. Once information is being "pushed out" through social media, families will come to expect information on some sort of schedule. As a rule, always let families know when you will provide new information via technology.
- Use the website/technology to reinforce your classroom learning and activities. Post a PowerPoint or video to the Web, if possible. Allow parents and families to download information that was pre-sented in class. Give parents the addresses of free information on the Web that will support your efforts. You might even try flipping your classroom for families!
- Invite feedback from parents and families about your website. Look at the statistical information to see how many visitors come to your site and what they look at while at your site.

7. Integrate families into lesson planning.

Create a lesson that engages families. Design a lesson over a day or two or, better yet, over a weekend that requires the student to engage their family in the material. Keeping family engagement in learning simple will encourage the disengaged to participate and build their confidence. Family integration into lesson planning does not have to occur every day or every week. Initially, set a goal to create four or five family lessons a year. The components of an integrated lesson are exactly the same as any lesson you would plan. The significant differences are (a) the lesson requires family participation, and (b) there is a mechanism for families to record and feed back their experiences to the teacher. Call a few of the parents or families you feel might be reluctant to participate and encourage them. Let them know that their contributions are essential elements in the learning life of their child.

8. Support the knowledge and skills of every family.

Having parents and families share their expertise is not a new concept in education. Unfortunately, there is less and less of this type of experiential learning because of limited time and the need to meet mastery objectives.

Determine knowledge and expertise held by the parents and families of students. Record that information for future use. Parents who work within the home can provide valuable resources to teachers. For example, skills like cooking can be incorporated into math lessons. A parent who is a house painter can support a geometry lesson by bringing a ladder to school and allowing the class to help determine the correct angle and placement of the ladder for its safe use. With the need to develop a 21st century workforce, engaging family knowledge has never been more critical.

Often, schools and classrooms gravitate to those parents who have interesting and exciting jobs. Remember though, every parent has value. Find that value and use it to support the learning that is taking place in the classroom.

9. Develop the efficacy of families.

Family efficacy is the notion that parents can help to produce positive educational outcomes with their child. Traditional avenues of parent involvement do not take into consideration building the capacity—the efficacy of parents—to transfer knowledge from school to their children. The most common place to improve family efficacy is to start with those activities already in place that are designed to promote learning outside of the classroom. Math nights, reading nights, and so forth all have value in helping families understand not only what their child needs to learn and master but, more importantly, how they can participate in their child's learning.

Even with the very best intentions of educators, attendance to these types of events is often sporadic. At times, just a handful of parents attend.

Schools report that when they do fill a room with parents, the parents of those students who are struggling are usually absent. To understand why this happens is to understand the role of family efficacy.

The improvements sought in these evening events are not to increase attendance but to make sure that the parents of the children who need the support are in attendance or are getting the support they need. Incorporate the following ideas into planned learning events for every family to improve the event and build efficacy in all parents and families.

- Use student work as a basis for parent learning
- Engage families in learning that they can then transfer to their children at home
- Take parental levels of education into consideration
- Incorporate the needs of families, such as language and childcare, into the meeting or workshop
- Consistently provide materials to families who could not attend

Parents and families need to know that they can play an important role in producing an effect with regard to their children's upbringing and education.

10. Believe that family engagement is essential.

Believing in family engagement speaks directly to the culture of the classroom and the school. Consider the following two statements made by a teacher and a parent:

Teacher: *Parents who want to be involved are involved. Those who don't are not. I can't spend any more time chasing ghosts. Many parents simply don't care enough to do the right thing, or they just check out. My job is to teach children, not their parents. We talk about this all the time at lunch and my colleagues agree with me. We can't handle one more thing.*

Parent: *At some point you just give up. I want to know what my son is doing, but I don't get any information. I get the report card, but by then it's too late. I want to help him, but I don't know how. I have asked and asked for help and now, well, they just think I am a troublemaker. You can only bang your head against the wall for so long, you know? The last time I went there I could see it on their faces that they didn't want me meddling in their school. I wanted a conference and they said OK, but half the teachers didn't come. I haven't been back since. I guess I will just pray that everything comes out all right.*

The statements above reflect what two people believe about the education of the same child. It is clear to the reader what each person believes and how they came to believe it. New actions that beget new results is an effective strategy to modify one's beliefs about issues and challenges.

All parents and families care about their children. On any given day, they may not express it in the manner we would wish, nor do they respond in ways that would help their children learn. However, parents and families are the first and most influential teachers of children. Believing that they choose to be disengaged will only serve to ensure that the struggles we face in successfully teaching all children will remain with us forever.

PRINCIPLE #3: EMPOWER EVERY FAMILY

Description. Families are recognized as essential members of the learning team for each student—their participation is welcomed, valued, and encouraged by the school. The school understands that families are important and influential resources, because they know their children best.

Where We Are

Based on the description, discuss and record where you think your school is today as it relates to the principle description.

3.1 The school makes a conscious effort to educate families to play a proactive role in the school life of their child throughout their school career.

Best Practice Description

As the school system and its component schools improve quality and performance, they too improve the neighborhoods and surrounding areas as better places for families to grow. All families have the tools necessary to assist their children with schoolwork and understand what their child needs to know in order to make continuous progress and meet high standards for achievement. Regardless of race, color, creed, or economic status, families feel a sense of efficacy toward helping their children and, in turn, a strong sense of loyalty to the school.

All school staff believes that families are integral to student performance and success and as such design student instruction with families in mind. Written communication about student learning is augmented with frequent conversations and strong relationships between teachers and families. Significant professional learning is devoted to empowering parents and families and leveraging family efficacy as a conduit to improved student achievement.

School staff work directly with families to ensure there are clear policies and procedures so that every family can participate, and voice opinions and concerns. Metrics are established to determine the effectiveness of family efficacy programs, and evaluation processes are in place to promote continuous improvement. The district and its component schools have in place a family mentoring program, supported with a budget and training so that families can directly assist other families in advocating for their child.

Use the Best Practice Description to Determine Your Present Performance Level

Practices in Place (Based on the Best Practice Description)

Practices to Be Implemented (Based on the Best Practice Description)

(Continued)

(Continued)

3.2 Families participate in the development of the student's learning plan, help assess progress, and provide support for their child's learning.

Best Practice Description

The school system and its component schools use a variety of school and community resources to ensure that every family understands what is expected academically from every child. Continuous communication of academic progress is available via conversation, written communication, and with the use of technology.

Family efficacy is promoted through a schoolwide commitment to outreach that includes the building of civic capacity, community engagement, home visits to families, and opportunities for parent leadership and advocacy development within the community. Outreach and extended learning activities are consistent and routine among all school staff. School strategic goals are written to measure the effectiveness and success of outreach activities designed to enhance school improvement.

The school is a critical partner with community agencies that foster a support mechanism for all families. Collaboration to provide parent training to support student learning is implemented and funded. Parent and family leaders, liaisons, and outreach staff continuously work to encourage engaged families to support the learning outcomes of all children.

Use the Best Practice Description to Determine Your Present Performance Level

Practices in Place (Based on the Best Practice Description)

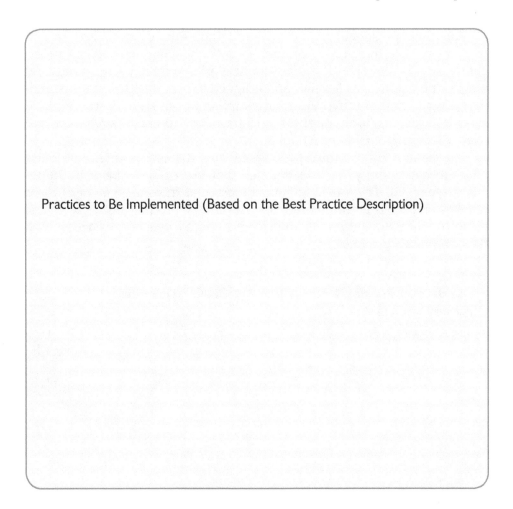

Practices to Be Implemented (Based on the Best Practice Description)

3.3 Teachers suggest mentoring possibilities and use their local knowledge, personal skills, assets, and networks in ways that support the school's program.

Best Practice Description

School staff are keenly aware that learning does not start and stop during the school day or at the schoolhouse door. Learning extended into the home is an expected and critical component in the construction and design of instructional methodology for all students, in all classrooms, by all teachers. All teachers successfully complete training to promote parental efficacy with outreach strategies and interactive lessons designed to engage parents in student learning.

Academic communication to parents and families includes a balance of student work that has been completed with a foreshadowing of the learning to take place and the work yet to be done so that all families can engage with future learning. All families have adequate information and understanding of the standards that their children are expected to meet.

All school personnel are inclusive of families in designing lessons and further promote the efficacy of families by enhancing their belief in their ability to assist their child with academic work. Workshops, meetings, and other opportunities for families are designed to promote their understanding of what their children are to accomplish in school and are provided specific resources, tools, support, and processes to encourage better and deeper learning outside of school.

All parents and families participate, and the school makes an extra effort to successfully include families that are or have been traditionally disengaged. There is tangible evidence that the engagement of these families and the promotion of their own efficacy produce better academic outcomes for their children. Families report high levels of satisfaction with their children's progress.

Use the Best Practice Description to Determine Your Present Performance Level

Practices in Place (Based on the Best Practice Description)

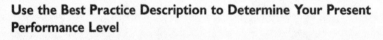

Practices to Be Implemented (Based on the Best Practice Description)

8

Principle #4

Engage Every Family in Decision Making

> *Public schools have become increasingly distant from the families of the children they serve, increasingly impersonal agents of a larger society.*
>
> —James Coleman

There is a great deal written on the importance of family engagement in governance and advocacy within the schools. Studies show that children of parents who are engaged in some aspects of school decision making have high levels of student achievement as well as more a more supportive community and public-at-large (Epstein et al., 2002; National PTA, 2000).

Dr. Joyce Epstein is unquestionably one of the nation's most prolific and most-often cited researchers in the field of family engagement. Dr. Epstein is the architect of the Six Types of Family Involvement and heads the National Network of Partnership Schools.

4 ENGAGE EVERY FAMILY IN DECISION MAKING

Principle #4: Engage Every Family in Decision Making

Description. The school recognizes the entitlement of families to be consulted and participate in decisions concerning their own children. The school is genuinely inclusive in its approach to decision making. It recognizes that this type of process creates a sense of shared responsibility among families, students, community members, educators and administrators.

4.1   The school creates opportunities for families to lead and participate in school learning, consultative, planning, social, and community events.

4.2   The school ensures that families and students have representation on the school's governing body and relevant decision-making groups.

Of the Six Types of Family Involvement, decision making is number five. Below is the language used by Dr. Epstein with regard to this particular type of involvement:

Decision Making—Type 5. The fifth type of parental involvement is decision making. Parents' voices must be heard when it comes to decision making at the school. This enables families to participate in decisions about the school's programs and activities that will impact their own and other children's educational experiences. All parents must be given opportunities to offer ideas and suggestions on ways to improve their schools. Having families as true stakeholders in the school creates feelings of ownership of the school's programs and activites. (National Network of Partnership Schools, n.d.)

Sample Activities

Examples of activities schools could conduct to promote decision making include but are not limited to

- encouraging parents to attend school improvement team meetings,
- assigning staff members to help parents address concerns or complaints,
- inviting staff and parent groups to meet collaboratively, providing space and time to do so,
- helping families advocate for each other, and
- involving parents in
  - planning orientation programs for new families,
  - developing parenting skills programs, and
  - hiring staff members.

PROBLEMS AND SOLUTIONS

Schools and districts should not only be aware of the input they receive from families but should send the clear message that the input is welcomed and valued. It is essential that the opinions and ideas reflect the diversity of a school population. Student opinions are also important at the secondary level. Schools are encouraged to promote student representation along with families in the decision-making process. The thoughts and ideas of all those participating must be trusted, respected, and heard.

Engaging parents and families in real decision making and school governance in many cases warrants a huge shift in the norms of school cultures. This shift includes a redefinition of roles, a changed belief system with regard to relationships with all, and a redistribution of power (Bauch & Goldring, 1995).

These changing roles of parents and families can have a significantly positive impact on the educational outcomes of all students (Wehlage, Smith, & Lipman, 1992). The roles of parents are expanding into new arenas; most notably, parents now are taking on the role of customer or consumer because of the rise in choices for their children's education. With these new roles, parents began to assume a greater voice in school governance and decision making.

Parents providing input into their children's education and exercising influence are the basic components of participation and empowerment, respectively (Bauch & Goldring, 1995). The involvement of families in the educational lives of their children has taken various turns and has been redefined over the years.

At the turn of the twentieth century, schools became more bureaucratic, espousing a "we-know-best" attitude and portraying educators as experts. This fundamental change in education began to significantly limit community influence over the school and limited further the influence of parents, especially those who were poor or those who were immigrants to the United States. The site-based management movement in education stressed a governance role of families to provide the best possible conditions for educating children (Havinghurst, 1972).

But, changing the role that families have historically held continues to be problematic. School councils, school improvement teams, and school correlate teams are different terms used to describe groups of people, usually administrators, teachers, parents, students, and at times, members of the community, to direct the strategic operation and improvement of a school.

At the inception, families involved in these types of committees rarely gave input on the important components of school success, that is, the budget, personnel, and programs (Bauch & Goldring, 1995). It seems that the reluctance of families to fully participate is directly related to their lack of understanding and information about school activities and school operations (Malen & Ogawa, 1988). Further, Malen and Ogawa (1988) cite parental discomfort in questioning professionals and the manner in which parents are invited or appointed to participate on the council.

When school administration selects families to participate, it is engaging in a not-so-subtle form of control that manifests itself as a search for families who will be unlikely to rock the boat. It stands to reason that the problematic nature of engaging families in school decision making is unquestionably related directly to their reluctance to disturb or, worse yet, violate the establish cultural norms of the school. Until this barrier is removed, it is unlikely that family engagement with governance and decision making will move far beyond token opportunities that provide few tangible results.

The inclusion of families in school decision making is an essential element for any school or district wishing to engage every family. To implement changes successfully, it is critical that all stakeholders have the opportunity to share in decisions about why changes are needed and how they are to be made (Kotter & Cohen, 2002). Research has found that changes which have involved or been led by families have resulted in significant achievements (Harris, 2009).

DeLaney (1997) has found that family involvement in school decision making must result in an overall satisfying experience or schools risk alienating the public and undermining their ongoing support for change.

Questions to Determine Effective Parent-Family Role in School Decision Making

1. Does your school/district truly value the input of all families?

2. Do you offer parent leadership training to build the capacity and efficacy for family engagement in decision making?

3. In what decisions do you (will you) engage families? Why? What decisions will not include families? Why?

4. How will you ensure that engagement in decision making is representative of all the families that your school serves?

WHERE WE ARE TODAY

In many cases, we have made great strides in understanding the importance of parental engagement, empowerment, and advocacy. Organizations like Project Appleseed and the Governor's Commonwealth Institute for Parent Leadership (GCIPL) (Pritchard Committee for Academic

Excellence, 2015) have created standards for parental involvement and include decision making as one of those important standards. The goal for parental involvement in decision making is to include parents in school decisions as well as developing parent leaders and representatives.

In their report *The Missing Piece of the Proficiency Puzzle*, the Kentucky Commissioner's Parent Advisory Council (2007) suggested that Kentucky become the first state in the nation to set standards for family and community engagement. Setting this standard involved creating six overarching objectives: (1) relationship building, (2) communications, (3) decision making, (4) advocacy, (5) learning opportunities, and (6) community partnerships. Within the objective devoted to decision making, the report encourages school staff to support and expect parents to be involved in school improvement decisions and to monitor and assist school improvement.

These are the very notions upon which the Five Simple Principles are built. The National PTA, developing its own set of parent involvement standards, clearly delineates the importance of parents as full partners in the decisions that affect all children and families (National PTA, 2000).

LET EVERY FAMILY HAVE A SAY

Parent involvement in school governance is a significant pillar in the site-based or school-based infrastructure. Whether through empowerment, advocacy, or participation, parents and families having a say in the opera-tion of their children's school and more importantly in their own child's education is a critical component in any listing of family engagement objectives for schools.

Whether through advocacy committees, traditional organizations—such as PTAs and other home-school groups—or school councils designed to lead the school through strategic planning and school improvement, family engagement with decision making and governance cannot be over-looked when designing a comprehensive set of standards to implement and measure the effectiveness of family participation in education.

Regardless if families volunteer, are appointed, or are elected, their involvement and, more importantly, their engagement with the strategic direction of the school is essential, not only for school improvement but for the improvement of the learning outcomes for all children.

A WORKING DEFINITION

A new standard definition incorporating family engagement in decision making, advocacy, and governance should encompass the simple concept of family engagement with the strategic (macro) direction of the school and the development, implementation, and evaluation of programs, policies, and practices (micro) within the school that impact the education of children within the school. From this definition, the standards can be developed.

It is important for families to know that their children attend a school that has adapted the philosophy of continuous improvement. Engaging families with strategic planning and goal setting is critical to this process. Families should be engaged with this process. School leaders should make ample time to share pertinent data and information about student achievement of the school in a format that all families can understand. For those parents who will have a direct responsibility for assisting with the strategic goal setting, training should be made available so that parents are equal partners when the time comes to review and analyze data and make recommendations for advancement.

The school council or school improvement team is essential to family engagement with governance. However, one committee limits the degree to which parents are engaged with school governance and strategic planning. School leaders and members of the council should expand the work of the main council by forming subgroups around the data, goals, and objectives of the strategic plan. These subgroups, similar in construction to the main council, act as an extension of the council, looking deeper into data, following implementation strategies closely, and looking for evidence of success to be reported to the community at-large.

HOW TO SELECT FAMILIES

Probably one of the most difficult challenges to engaging families in this type of governance is finding enough parents willing to give of their time and then ensuring that the parents doing the work are representative of the entire community. Further, you may find yourself in a situation of trying to convince a family that their participation and opinions are indeed valued and necessary. While many family engagement standards are inclusive of the notion that a wide variety of parents and families must be involved, there is little guidance as to how to create a representative pool of parents. Failure to implement a system that ensures all parents are represented runs the risk of a certain type or class of parents being involved in all aspects. This actually moves to further disengage those parents who are already disengaged from the school.

Geographic Representation

The first option open to school leaders and councils is to study the geography and population of the school attendance area. Most district offices can provide an analysis of where families live and the concentration of families within neighborhoods and regions. Often, transportation maps and student pick-up plans can provide great data to determine where families live. Knowing this information helps to balance the representation, much like the census does in establishing senate and congressional districts. The fictitious example below represents this approach to engaging parents in governance:

Anytown Elementary School

Student population: 800

Number of parents/families needed to fill council/committees: 30

Neighborhood	Number of Families	Percentage of Whole	Number of Representatives
Barron Estates	150	19	6
West Village	200	25	8
East Village	50	6.2	2
City Apartments	260	32.4	9
Mount Pleasant	50	6.2	2
Amberton Valley, Links Estates, Rural Families	90	11.2	3
Total	800	100	30

(Percentages rounded and adjusted)

When looking for parents and families to participate in various school governance councils, this simple chart can guide the efforts to recruit. Representatives can go to homeowner associations, apartment complex committees, and so forth, to share why the school needs the assistance and how the engagement of families from this particular area will be proportionally representative of the families that the school serves.

For cities and rural areas, maps can be drawn and divided by quadrants or other ways to garner representative support. Local high school math classes might welcome the real-life math problem to help their own school or neighboring schools.

Ethnic Representation

The very same process as identified above can also work if schools wish to divide parent participation by ethnicity and race in those schools that are significantly diverse. A stratification of the above two charts can even provide a more pinpointed approach to parent engagement by not only determining the neighborhood or area but also using the multicultural aspects of the areas to ensure that parents are geographically represented as is their ethnicity, nationality, and race.

These representatives then can become ambassadors for their neighborhoods and areas. The school frequently publishes (with consent) the names, addresses, and contact information of family participants so that any family that may have a question, concern, or idea understands there is a representative just for them. These ambassadors can also hold neighborhood meetings, parent coffees, and so forth, to help all families understand the information being created with regard to the strategic plan and vision of the school.

GETTING BACK TO THE TIP OF THE SPEAR

Consistent adherence to this type of process is culture changing. Over time as the expectations, beliefs, and values of all stakeholders change, the processes will get easier, largely because they become engrained into the fabric of the school. Regardless of leadership or committee changes, the process will be intact for years to come.

School administrators spend a great deal of time working with families who raise concerns and objections to issues that occur within the context of the school day. From academic issues (why did my son get a zero?) to behavioral issues (why was my son suspended for three days?) to school climate issues (I think my daughter's clothes are appropriate and are not suggestive!) administrators spend an inordinate amount of time helping families through the maze of policies, procedures, and practices within the school.

This time away from the "tip of the spear" of school leadership—the focus on student performance and school improvement—is a symptom of a larger problem. Administrators often lament that the time to focus on instructional issues is significantly reduced because of these "other" noninstructional issues. Developing customer understanding and loyalty toward the policies that govern the school and the procedures and practices that allow the school to function each day is rooted in the degree to which parents and families are engaged *from the beginning* or, better yet, *before the beginning*.

When processes that cultivate family understanding and loyalty are touted as a conduit to success, often school personnel have the same reaction: We have no time to do that. As the late Stephen Covey taught us, we have choices as people to focus on what is urgent or what is important. It seems reasonable to understand that spending the time to cultivate understanding and loyalty to a school and its procedures saves a great deal of time devoted to problem-solving, family distress, and negative catalysts that ultimately cause school-family relationships to be severely limited or, worse yet, destroyed.

Using effective communication for family feedback (surveys, focus groups, web sites, flyers, parent organizations, etc.), school personnel can engage a significant portion of the population. Below is an example of how to engage and build understanding and loyalty toward a school policy, procedure, or practice.

AN EXAMPLE OF FAMILY GOVERNANCE IN ACTION

The Anytown High School Tardy Policy

Data from Anytown High School suggests a growing problem with the numbers of students either late to school or arriving late to classes throughout the day. Five-year data indicates a 25% increase in the numbers of students tardy to school or class.

The data has been disaggregated further to show that the problem is more pronounced with students in the ninth grade and the rate of tardiness among minority students outpaces that of the majority students. The principal of Anytown has decided to take the issue to the school council to develop a new more stringent tardy policy.

The scenario above is fairly common among schools. Analyzing data discovers a problem, and the school leadership along with the council wishes to resolve the problem. In most cases, there would be discussion in the council of how the tardy policy can be strengthened so that the problem is diminished or resolved.

The administration develops a new plan, brings it to the council for approval, and once approved, the policy is implemented for the following school year. While this process seems sound, it did not engage enough families in the policies, procedures, and practices of the school, and as such, when the policy is enacted, the administration is in for a large contingent of angry students and families who will be caught off guard by the change.

A better more productive way is to elicit information from students and families in a meaningful way so that the new policy is truly representative of the thoughts and ideas of the entire community. Steps toward this enhanced process might include the following:

- Parent ambassadors host community (neighborhood) meetings to share the information.
- Information is shared via homeowner or neighborhood e-mail lists.
- Focus groups conducted by representatives of the school council are implemented to garner information and opinions.
- Students who have been offenders of the policy are interviewed to determine the root causes of the tardiness.

- Information collected is collated and reviewed by the committee to determine if it is policy that needs to be changed or if there are practices that can be changed that would resolve the problem.
- The results are effectively communicated through numerous vehicles long before the policy, procedure, or practice is put into effect.
- The council and subcommittees put into place mechanisms to monitor and provide feedback during the initial inception of the new policy to determine effectiveness.

Research and practice agree that there are a number of tangible strategies that when employed with fidelity, increase family engagement with school decision making and allow every family to have a voice in the education of their children.

Attention to how families are invited to participate in school governance and decision-making activities is critical. Attention to ethnic, social, and economic diversity is important when setting the stage to allow every family to have a voice. Professional learning that includes families, families who mentor or adopt other families, and varied measures of collecting information all lend themselves well to creating a culture that demonstrates a strong commitment to reaching beyond the few families that are traditionally engaged.

Most important is the clear idea that parents and families are welcomed and valued as part of the school decision-making process. Building the capacity of families in decision making ensures that in time, every family will have a voice.

CASE STUDY: THE UNIFORM POLICY

David Marks was the brand new principal at River Crest Middle School. David was new to the school and new to the school district, having worked as an assistant principal in a district over 200 miles from his new school. At David's former school, a strict uniform policy was in place to which all students were required to comply. Students had their choice of a few colors of shirts and were required to wear khaki pants or, for girls, knee-length skirts. There was assistance in acquiring uniforms for families in need.

David's first order of business at River Crest was to garner support for a uniform policy. He knew that uniforms reduced misbehavior in school and had a profound effect on homework completion rates and test scores. He also had data to prove his assertions. He wanted to be sure that the same level of success could be generated at River Crest as had been at his previous school.

River Crest student achievement had been declining in recent years. The school had seen enrollment growth beyond its functional capacity and a significant shift in the demographics of the student population. River Crest had been in the process of being identified as a Title I school when its previous principal decided to retire. David knew that he had his work cut out for him and also believed that getting the uniform policy in place was a key ingredient in his plan for success.

During the first days of summer and brand new on the job, David gathered the school improvement team for a meeting. The team consisted of a few teachers who were team leaders at the school, the assistant principal, the guidance counselor, and three parents. One of the parents was the president of the PTA, and the other two parents were recruited to serve on the committee by the previous principal. Decisions regarding school processes, policies, and procedures were first discussed at the School Improvement Team meetings and, if agreement existed, taken to the faculty and the PTA for feedback.

David did an excellent job of pitching his idea of school uniforms. The Improvement Team was actually excited about the idea and pledged their full support. David wondered aloud to the group if the policy could start in the fall. No one saw why not. There was plenty of time left in the summer to communicate the policy to families and for families to prepare.

The teachers on the School Improvement Team sent a survey to all staff to gather input on the new uniform policy. Concurrently, the PTA president sent an e-mail to all members of the PTA who had given their e-mail addresses. The remaining parents vowed to share the information with "other parents" as well. The incoming class of sixth-grade students and their families were not on any e-mail lists. David promised to send a letter to all of those parents explaining the process of developing this new policy.

Within a week or so, David received excellent news. Over 85% of the school staff was in favor of the new uniform policy. The PTA president reported that the overwhelming majority of people who responded to her e-mail were also in favor of the new policy. The two parents on the committee in addition to the PTA president reported that "everyone we talked to loved the idea." David was thrilled. His first goal had been completed. At the beginning of the next week, with over eight weeks left of the summer before school started, David sent out a letter introducing himself as the new principal and outlining the expectations for the new uniform policy that was to take effect when school started in the upcoming fall.

As David's letters started arriving at homes and were read by parents, the River Crest phones went on overload. The secretaries could not keep up with the calls coming in to complain about the new uniform policy. Parents were angry, and some were somewhat hostile on the phone with staff. Within a few hours, David had over 100 phone messages to return. At the same time, numerous parents took to Facebook, and the comments were not positive or supportive. David watched in disbelief as the number of "likes" for the comment "Get rid of the new principal and the uniforms" added up right in front of his eyes. An anti-uniform campaign had already been organized and was being disseminated through Facebook and Twitter. Hundreds of parents were attaching their support to ensure that this policy never materialized.

At the summer school board meeting, over fifty River Crest parents were in attendance. Many spoke to the school board about the unfairness of the policy and being "blindsided" by the new principal. Parents demanded the superintendent and/or school board members step in and, in the words of one parent, "stop this madness." The superintendent contacted David the next morning to discuss the matter.

(Continued)

(Continued)

David was dumbfounded. He explained that he understood the process for policy changes at the school and had followed it precisely. A survey was sent to faculty and parents and all the information came back supportive. The superintendent indicated that the district communications office had now confirmed that opposition to the policy far outweighed the support. David was told to put a hold on his policy until he could demonstrate support in the community for it.

David's happiness was short lived. Barely the principal for one month, he had already created a problem that landed at the doorstep of the school board and superintendent. His School Improvement Team members tried to cheer David up and let him know that they would help him get the support he needed. David was privately thinking that he had made a terrible mistake accepting this new job.

Questions

1. David followed the school process for new policies. Why did things go wrong?

2. With all of the initial feedback coming back so positive and supportive, how did David miss the overwhelming negative reaction?

3. Why did so many families react so negatively? What were they negative about?

4. How could David have better understood his community before launching his new policy?

5. Given what you have learned about family engagement in governance and decision making, what could have been done differently to avoid the confrontation?

PRINCIPLE #4: ENGAGE EVERY FAMILY IN DECISION MAKING

Description. The school recognizes the entitlement of parents to be consulted and participate in decisions concerning their own children. The school is genuinely inclusive in its approach to decision making. It recognizes that this type of process creates a sense of shared responsibility among families, students, community members, and educators.

Where We Are

Based on the description, discuss and record where you think your school is today as it relates to the principle description.

4.1 The school creates opportunities for families to lead and participate in school learning, consultative, planning, social, and community events.

Best Practice Description

The school has developed, implemented, and evaluated an extensive network of opportunities for families to learn and be engaged with their children's learning as well as decisions that affect their children, and has an effective public relations plan to ensure that every family understands the opportunities open to them. Families are invited to participate in training and professional learning programs for teachers and other staff and have specific professional learning programs designed for them.

There are systems in place for participation in strategic planning and rules and procedures development, and data shows a significantly high level of family engagement. The school creates mechanisms for feedback prior to acting or implementing programs or practices that will affect children and their families. The school is dedicated to a system of strategic communication that frames issues and ideas for families and thoughtfully engages them to solicit feedback, ideas, and opinions.

The school understands its role as a community learning center; the school works in tandem with families to ensure that school goals and environment are reflective of family input and opinion. The school/district hosts social and community events, in different parts of the district, and is inclusive of all families in the events with detailed attention toward language, culture, and demographic issues. Data collected by the school indicate a high satisfaction and engagement rate among all families regarding their ability to become involved and immersed in learning, planning, and events.

Use the Best Practice Description to Determine Your Present Performance Level

Practices in Place (Based on the Best Practice Description)

Practices to Be Implemented (Based on the Best Practice Description)

4.2 The school ensures that families and students have representation on the school's governing body and relevant decision-making groups.

Best Practice Description

The leadership and staff of the school and district believe that a platform of shared decision making is critical to creating an environment of continuous improvement and, as such, allows for numerous vehicles by which every family can have a say in the decisions made within the individual schools and at the district level. Not only have policies and procedures been put into place at the system level, but monies are budgeted to ensure sufficient training supports quality processes.

The culture of the organization has shifted and has redefined the roles of families, created a changed belief system with regard to building and maintaining effective relationships to promote shared decision making, and redistributed power to allow for families to partner in the governance of the schools, including budget and school improvement issues. The district understands the role of families as customer and consumer and has in place systems and metrics to determine the needs of its customers and involve its customers in decisions that affect the overall operation and governance of the school.

Every school within the district has a council on which family representatives participate. Schools have ensured through a well-defined process that all neighborhoods and geographical areas within the attendance zone are represented on the council and that there is a mechanism in place to establish how parents and families will be appointed and what length of time they will serve. Interpreters and materials translated into native languages are available.

Whether the council is advisory in nature or has voting and operational rights or control, at the center is the belief of the school system and its employees that families have a voice in decision making and governance. Mechanisms are also in place to garner the opinions of families or the community-at-large when decisions are being discussed and considered.

Families participating on decision-making councils report that their participation is authentic; they feel a significant value in the process and report to a wide range of families on the work of the council. A mechanism of family mentorship is in place to ensure quality participation is continually maintained.

Use the Best Practice Description to Determine Your Present Performance Level

Practices in Place (Based on the Best Practice Description)

(Continued)

(Continued)

Practices to Be Implemented (Based on the Best Practice Description)

9

Principle #5

Engage the Greater Community

THE POWER OF COMMUNITY

For a moment, consider the following ideas adapted from Decker, Decker, Boo, Gregg, and Erickson (2001):

Consideration 1: Approximately 75% of the U.S. public do not have school-age children and have no contact with the nation's public schools.

Consideration 2: The diverse mix of students served by public schools continues to grow and change.

Consideration 3: Resources to public schools are shrinking.

Consideration 4: The public's faith in public institutions and the government in general is fading, creating more skepticism.

Consideration 5: There is growing governmental support for alternatives to public education.

Assuming you affirm that the majority of these considerations are true, then what do we as

---

Principle #5: Engage the Greater Community

Description. The school places a strong focus on building and creating partnerships external to the school. The school recognizes the strengths and talents that exist in the communities that influence student learning and development and seeks to use these to strengthen and support the school, students, and their families. It also recognizes that the school can be a focal point for communities to come together and engage in capacity building and renewal. The school views itself as an important community asset and has community representatives on the school's governing body. There is a clear recognition from the school that the greater community plays an integral role in the educational success of the school.

5.1 Partnerships are made with individuals and organizations in work and community places to take on mentoring roles within student internship and work placement programs. The partnerships also have a role to play within other activities, such as community-based learning projects, guest speaker programs, job shadows, apprenticeship opportunities, and tutors.

5.2 Partnerships are made with other learning institutions—other schools, technical colleges, universities, and other training providers in order for students to pursue learning opportunities, build their skills, and achieve learning credentials.

5.3 Opportunities evolve from the school for creating and implementing adult-learning and community development courses to be run within the school building.

---

educators propose to do about it? The opening of the book underscored the need for educators to reach beyond the walls of schools and engage families and communities. What is needed now more than ever are homes, communities, and schools working together to both champion and improve public education.

The quality of connections between children's education and the community that surrounds that education is a significant component in the successful education of every child (Christenson & Sheridan, 2001). For those community partnerships to be effective, there must exist a keen understanding of the cultural, socioeconomic, health, social, and recreational needs and interests of each school's families. Family literacy programs, health services, English as a second language programs, and vocational training programs are all examples of community-based programs that support families, which in turn supports the education of children (Espinosa, 1995).

Experts and researchers in the field of community engagement provide advice on building partnerships between schools and community groups and agencies. Experts agree that conceptualizing the role of the partnership and then planning for the partnership are essential first steps with the planning phase often cited as the most important step.

The school principal and the community need to work together on establishing goals, assessing needs, developing a vision, and deciding management issues. Evaluating the effectiveness of the partnerships as well as the outcomes identified by the partnerships are also essential if partnerships are to succeed and persevere (Gretz, 2003).

Points to Ponder

1. How do you presently engage the community in your classroom/school/ district?

2. How does that engagement translate into student learning?

3. How can you enhance community engagement to support learning for all students?

COMMUNITY SCHOOLS AND ASSET MAPPING

A community school is both a place and a set of partnerships where an integrated focus on academics, services, supports, and opportunities leads to improved student learning, stronger families, and healthier communities. Using public schools as a hub, community schools knit together inventive, enduring relationships among educators, families, community volunteers, and community partners—businesses, family support groups, health and social service agencies, youth development organizations, community organizations, and other organizations— committed to children. They act in concert to transform traditional schools—permanently—into partnerships for excellence. Because individual schools and the school system join forces with community agencies and organizations to operate community schools, schools are not left to work alone (Blank, Melaville, & Shah 2003).

THE ADVANTAGES OF COMMUNITY SCHOOLS

Supporters of community education understand the advantages of community-based educational opportunities and the social capital that is created with partnerships between schools and the communities they serve. Being able to build a better and stronger capacity for helping students achieve at their highest levels is at the core of why educators need to embrace the concept of community schools. Involving communities provides access to additional resources and opportunities for school environments and programs that meet the needs of all students, not just some students. Developing students in an academic venue has been a core process of public education from its inception.

A community school not only develops academic proficiencies but inspires students to learn and grow in nonacademic venues as well. This marriage produces the landscape within which all students can learn at high levels. Lastly, the idea of social capital, reinforced and enhanced by connecting students to the community, is now a source of learning and exploration.

As presented by Kretzmann and McKnight (1993), community asset mapping is a capacity-focused way of redeveloping communities. This positive approach is proposed as a substitute for the traditional deficits focus on a community's needs and problems. Using problems to formulate human service interventions, the authors maintain, targets resources to service providers rather than residents, fragments efforts to provide solutions, places reliance on outside resources and outside experts, and leads to a maintenance and survival mentality rather than to community development.

Instead, they propose the development of policies and activities based on an understanding or "map" of the community's resources—individual capacities and abilities and organizational resources with the potential for promoting personal and community development. This "mapping" is designed to promote connections or relationships between individuals, between individuals and organizations, and between organizations and organizations.

The asset-based approach, the authors maintain, does not remove the need for outside resources but makes their use more effective. The community assets approach

- Starts with what is present in the community
- Concentrates on the agenda-building and problem-solving capacity of the residents
- Stresses local determination, investment, creativity, and control

In this context, spatial mapping may or may not be used. Within any given neighborhood or community, most assets as defined by Kretzmann and McKnight (1993) do not have a spatial quality. Community asset mapping has very little to do with spatial mapping and much more to do with a community survey and the mobilizing of individuals and organizations to make connections and build capacity.

The information obtained through the survey process must be organized and accessed in an inventory format. It can be computerized as a database inventory. Computerized mapping can be used, showing the location of assets on a geographic map as well as the attributes attached to each asset.

The community asset mapping process is intended to initiate a process that will fully mobilize a community to use its assets around a vision and

a plan to solve its own problems. Their guidebook provides considerable detail about how this might be accomplished, with numerous examples of the types of connections that can be developed.

Assets Map: Possible Components

An asset map can include all or any portion of the ideas presented below, depending on the needs of the school or school district. Map, collect, and discuss your findings.

Geographic representation (may look more like a map)

- Geographic features (i.e., rivers, mountains, etc.)
- Demographic (i.e., population density areas)
- Features (i.e., highways, businesses)
- Other

Broad categories (create lists)

- Resources (services, businesses, faith groups, clubs)
- Attributes (geographic, people power, etc.)
- Opportunities (coming soon, could be, and what ifs)
- Needs/concerns (problems, gaps, etc.)
- Other

Social capital resources (list or matrix—name, service/product, consumer population)

- Health and human services organizations
- Public and private
- Cultural groups (library, museum, etc.)
- Foundations
- Faith-based organizations
- Service clubs
- Social and fraternal groups
- Schools
- Recreation programs
- Businesses
- Manufacturers, retailers, large and small
- Other

School district (may be lists and graphs)

- Assets
- Concerns
- Demographics
- Population of municipalities in district
- Racial/cultural breakdown

(Continued)

(Continued)

- Predominate languages
- Student proficiency level/test scores
- Community support
- Other

How can this information garner community support for your school?

Activity: Community Asset Mapping Made Simple

Step One

Put together your focus team (I like the word team rather than group because it translates into teamwork). The team should include an administrator, teacher, community rep, parent, student, PTA parent, businessperson, park and recreation rep., and so forth. Provide as much diversity as possible when forming your asset mapping team.

Step Two

Supply the group with a three by five foot or enlarged attendance area map, laminated, and if possible, framed onto corkboard. Provide each team member with color-coded pushpins and some round label tags (like you use on a key ring).

Step Three

Ask your team to define assets and then brainstorm assets in your community. Assets can include but are not limited to things like parks, health clinics and hospitals, skate parks, community services or agencies, potential partners, or anything the group sees as an asset for their community. Once the team identifies all of the potential assets within the school community, the team can partner up and canvas a portion of the attendance area, interview someone from the facility, get a flyer, and write a short statement on what is offered at that facility.

Step Four

Color code the asset map (example: blue is for health clinics. . . . Take a blue pushpin and number the facility on the white tab).

Step Five

Construct a small write-up about that facility, hours, services, and so forth.

Step Six

Translate the write-ups into the languages of the school and put them in an online database that can be shared and updated as necessary. If possible, create an e-version of your map and hyperlink it to the color-coded assets in your community. Of course there is always the tried and true old-fashioned way of putting everything into a notebook!

THE START OF AN ASSET MAP

Below is a depiction of what the start of an asset map might look like:

Community Asset Map

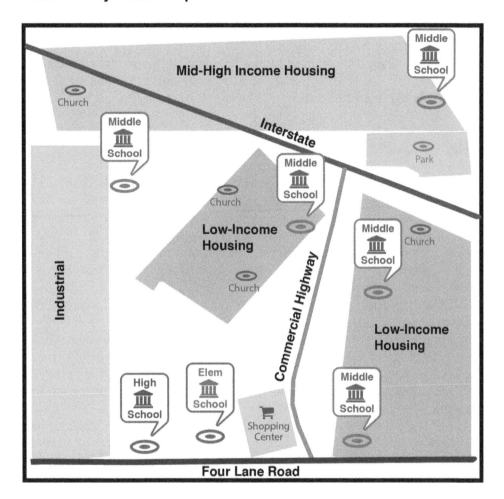

This map, which can be considerably more detailed, notes the following:

- The location of schools
- The location of churches, parks, and shopping
- The location of types of neighborhoods
- The location of roads, main thoroughfares, and highways
- The location of non-residential areas

Here are a few questions that the asset map might help answer. Remember to consider the non-spatial applications of assets:

- What challenges may be inherent to this district?
- What challenges may be inherent to the individual schools?
- What kinds of engagement challenges do you think the schools have?
- What community resources are available and how could they be used to support the schools?
- What other information might be good to know that should be added to this map? In other words, what don't you know that you probably need to know?

THE IDEA OF COLLECTIVE IMPACT

A new type of capital can also be produced when various community agencies and groups abandon their individual agendas in favor of "a collective approach to improving student achievement" (Kania & Kramer, 2011, p. 36). The notion of collective impact is a commitment of a group of specific actors from various sectors of the community to work together in creating a common agenda or solving a specific social problem (Kania & Kramer, 2011).

The successful example of this process is *Project Strive*, which seems to be making a difference with regard to education in Cincinnati, Ohio. In many communities, the impact of the engagement of separate community agencies brings about isolated impacts to schools and thus rarely creates the change sought. Strive and projects like it are said to be turning the tide with regard to engaging the greater community to support student learning.

Leaders looking to make a true difference for education adapt a holistic approach to reform, realizing that trying to repair one aspect of a child's educational experience, such as after-school programs, will not have the desired long-term effect unless all of the necessary components improved simultaneously (Kania & Kramer, 2011).

The textbook definition for collective impact states "the commitment of a group of important actors from different sectors to a common agenda for solving a specific social problem" (Kania & Kramer, 2011, p. 36).

HOW COMMUNITY CONNECTIONS CAN HELP

Minority students now make up 42 percent of public school enrollment (Kena et al., 2014). In the vast majority of schools that have seen a rise in minority students, many because of the surge of Latino and Hispanic students, the students themselves often lag behind. According to the National Assessment of Educational Practice (NAEP) low-achieving youngsters accounted for 37.6 percent of students scoring in the lowest quintile (Flanagan & Grissmer, 2002). Price (2008) suggests there are a number of challenges with which community engagement can help, such as closing the gap of what students know and need to know, dropping out, student disengagement, and the gap in higher education attainment.

With all of this evidence, why is it that community engagement with schools is overlooked by educators as a primary strategy by which to combat low student achievement? Some would argue that most teachers and administrators are educated to think of themselves as individual leaders of classrooms, schools, or districts, with little attention to the importance of teamwork and collaborations with parents, community partners, and others interested in students' success in school.

Colleges and universities have been slow to change required curricula to incorporate the preparation of teacher and leadership candidates to work with families, and communities have been slow to respond as well (McBride, 1991). Epstein and Sanders (2006) surveyed 161 colleges and universities and found, while some progress has been made with regard to this issue, much work needed to be done to ensure that educators emerging from preparation programs could act as catalysts and effectively foster collaborative partnerships that supported all children.

THE NECESSARY INGREDIENTS FOR SUCCESSFUL COMMUNITY ENGAGEMENT

In order for partnerships to be effective, four factors need to be present to allow schools to build successful linkages and relationships with community groups and agencies that result in improved learning for all students (Sanders & Harvey, 2002). The school's commitment to learning, the principal's support and vision for community involvement, the school's receptivity and openness to community involvement, and the school's willingness to engage in two-way communication are all important ingredients.

Today, the term *professional learning community* is well established in U.S. schools. Epstein and Salinas (2004) offer a new term, the *school learning community*, as a stronger alternative. The authors make the following comparison between professional learning communities and school learning communities:

A professional learning community emphasizes the teamwork of principals, teachers, and staff to identify school goals, improve curriculum and instruction, reduce teachers' isolation, assess student progress, and increase the effectiveness of school programs. Professional teamwork is important and can greatly improve teaching, instruction, and professional relationships in a school, but it falls short of producing a true community of learners. In contrast, a school learning community includes educators, students, parents, and community partners who work together to improve the school and enhance students' learning opportunities. (p. 12)

As is the case with other authors and researchers, Epstein and Salinas suggest action teams made up of the internal and external constituents listed above and well-crafted action plans to plan, implement, and evaluate successful school learning communities. Organizationally, educators, parents, and other partners work together to strengthen and maintain their community involvement programs over time. These partners also recognize that they all have roles to play in helping students succeed in school.

THE BENEFITS OF ENGAGING THE COMMUNITY

Schools continue to struggle with issues that act as barriers to allowing all students to be successful in school. Engaging and connecting with the greater community and developing strong, measurable partnerships with them provides successful academic dividends to all children.

Attendance

Epstein and Sheldon (2002) found that schools are more likely to improve student attendance and reduce chronic absenteeism with three broad strategies: (a) taking a comprehensive approach to attendance with activities that involve students, families, and the community; (b) using more positive involvement activities than negative or punishing activities; and (c) sustaining a focus on improving attendance over time. Schools that conduct a variety of activities that involve students, parents, and community partners see increases in favorable attendance.

Supporting Language Minority Students

Language minority students suffer a mismatch between the language and culture of their schools and those they experience at home and in their community (Adger & Locke, 2000). The more schools establish programs with community-based organizations, the more likely language minority students will prosper and learn in their local schools. Adgar and Locke (2000) suggest that a few partnerships have made radical changes in elementary schooling and at the secondary school level; partnerships often use traditional methods of assisting students academically, such as tutoring students in the academic areas, supporting English language development, and organizing programs to promote students' leadership skills and higher education goals. But they also address social factors that may interfere with students' achievement. For example, the Filipino Youth Empowerment program directly targets gang participation as a risk factor. This partnership also offers innovative services, such as bridging gaps between immigrant parents and their Americanized children. In secondary schools, partnerships are apt to work with existing school structures without altering them significantly, although this is not always the case.

Several recommendations are made to foster these important collaborations, including commitment by both parties and the need to start small and build the partnership. Research summaries clearly show that language minority students benefit from school and community-based partnerships.

After-School Programs

It is important that the after-school program staff understand and link their efforts to the school curriculum. Henderson, Mapp, Johnson, and Davies (2007) share steps to ensure the proper curricular alignment between after-school programs and schools (p. 107):

- Encourage after-school program staff and teachers to observe each other at work, and share ideas and information about the students.
- Invite program staff to attend professional development sessions to update and build their teaching skills.
- Inform program staff about the school's curriculum and learning programs (especially math and reading).
- Exchange textbooks, assignments, and learning materials.
- Share the school's data on student achievement and other outcomes.

Authors and researchers repeatedly underscore the need to link student learning to programs and activities that support in-school learning. This type of work also leads to building a more successful and broader base of engagement for families by connecting them to others in the community.

Successful partnerships can emanate from just about anywhere: committed leadership, teachers, and community supporters and/or activists. The challenge to all educators is not to carve up responsibilities between a shrinking roll of educators but to look to their communities for the resources necessary and reconceptualize the role of schools and their relationships to communities, such that the education of every child is enhanced. The relationship between a community and its public schools must be strengthened if the schools wish lasting success for every child.

ADDITIONAL BENEFITS OF
SCHOOL-COMMUNITY PARTNERSHIPS

In addition to the return on investment already discussed, there are other benefits from exploring and building partnerships with community groups, agencies, and businesses. Partnerships increase the likelihood that community members become more knowledgeable and aware of school environment and performance and can give better input and support as a result of this knowledge. Community members gain a better appreciation and understanding of the larger social, economic, and cultural demands placed on the schools, students, and their families.

In an era of decreasing revenue and increased scrutiny of the expenditure of taxpayer funds, community partnerships help those outside of the schools see the wise and efficient expenditure of funds and garner a better understanding of how and why money is spent.

Community partnerships provide important mentorships to students and give students first-hand engagement with positive role models, increasing the odds for student success in school. Providing mentorships and working directly with schools offers community members the intrinsic satisfaction of knowing the positive differences they have made in the lives of children.

Business partners can be a valuable source of information and opportunity for students and staff. Providing real-world experiences, such as internships, apprenticeships and a better understanding of career and job opportunities, is invaluable to schools as they work with students on future plans. Educators gain important insights into the world or workforce demands, and students gain a better appreciation for the opportunities that may exist after high school graduation. In some cases, schools receive financial support for program implementation, student counseling, and career development.

DESIGNING COMMUNITY ENGAGEMENT

One of the most significant challenges to community engagement with schools is the ability for those within the school or district to conceptualize exactly what the engagement looks like and, more importantly, what will occur as a result of the engagement. Often, educators instinctively know that community engagement can have a positive impact on their school and rush to garner that engagement, only to find that it is short lived. The biggest barrier to successful engagement is the lack of conceptualizing what it actually is.

Recently, I was introduced to a concept that I found very exciting: *Design Thinking*. While I had heard these terms before, it was only after a few presentations that I understood fully the power of the Design Thinking process. Design Thinking has been used successfully in industry and business to develop innovative solutions to complex problems. Design Thinking emerged out of the work of designers in the fields of product design and engineering.

Design, in its most effective form, is really a process or an action less a result. Design Thinking is really an operational title or definition to a process for designing solutions to ambiguous problems or, in other words, a problem-solving protocol. Often, conceptualizing and creating pathways for community engagement can be ambiguous and daunting. The process, similar to other improvement processes, allows for a group to work through the various steps in order to create a desired result. Following are the steps in the Design Thinking process:

Discovery: Discovery allows participants to gain insights into the needs and the problem being addressed.

Define the problem: The define step is a way to ensure we really understand the problem. By refining and acquiring feedback, the problem can be either refined or revised based on the input.

Create and consider many options: This is the fun, creative part of the design thinking process. This step allows participants to start with the preverbal "blank slate" and create a volume of ideas in both words and pictures.

Refine and evaluate: Any good process for discovery of improved outcomes has an evaluation component. Participants often ask themselves what they like about the ideas created or what they don't like about the ideas. This is also an opportunity to ask questions and seek clarification and suggestions on the work already accomplished. Once this step in finished, go back and begin to refine the solution(s) to the problem. Evaluation without refinement usually ends up killing good ideas.

Note that the steps above may need to be repeated until such time that the correct answers become obvious.

Solve (execute): At some point, however, the group is satisfied that they have created a solution to their problem. Pick the best idea and execute!

The next page gives you an opportunity to try out the Design Thinking process for yourself. Think about a challenge in your school that community engagement and support could help support. Maybe it's reading levels or discipline issues. Use the data and improvement plans that exist within your school to determine a challenge that could be improved through thoughtful community engagement and use the Design Thinking model to achieve an idea that can be implemented.

Discovery: Discuss, interview, research, dig, and find information about the reason a change is needed and why or how community engagement will play a role.

Define the problem: What is the problem to be solved? Define it; get feedback on it; revise it.

Create and consider many options: Generate solutions to the problem. Get creative!

Refine and evaluate: Clarify, refine, and hone in on the solution.

Solve and execute: State the process to be implemented that allows community engagement to address a challenge.

PRINCIPLE #5: ENGAGE THE GREATER COMMUNITY

Description. The school places a strong focus on building and creating partnerships external to the school. The school recognizes the strengths and talents that exist in the communities that influence student learning and development and seeks to use these to strengthen and support the school, students, and their families. It also recognizes that the school can be a focal point for communities to come together and engage in capacity building and renewal. The school views itself as an important community asset and has community representatives on the school's governing body. There is a clear recognition from the school that the greater community plays an integral role in the educational success of the school.

Where We Are

Based on the description, discuss and record where you think your school is today as it relates to the principle description.

5.1 Partnerships are made with individuals and organizations in work and community places to take on mentoring roles within student internship and work placement programs. The partnerships also have a role to play within other activities, such as community-based learning projects, guest speaker programs, job shadows, apprenticeship opportunities, and tutors.

Best Practice Description

The school system as well as the individual schools have developed strong two-way and effective partnerships with numerous business and civic organizations to support the learning needs and outcomes of all students within the district and individual schools. Schools have been encouraged to and have also developed similar meaningful partnerships that are designed to specifically support their unique or individual needs.

The district and its component schools value the participation of adult community members in the education of its students, and as a result, numerous opportunities to connect learning to the community are evident. Individual needs, such as tutoring, learning and service projects, job shadowing, apprenticeships, guest speaker programs, and other community-based programs are evident in schools.

The district along with community partners has focused on the needs of students and can track and measure the results of the efforts. The district and its partners have also developed and implemented an effective process of ensuring that the community-at-large understanding of the opportunities available for partnership and the support of student learning outcomes.

Use the Best Practice Description to Determine Your Present Performance Level

Practices in Place (Based on the Best Practice Description)

Practices to Be Implemented (Based on the Best Practice Description)

5.2 Partnerships are made with other learning institutions—other schools, technical colleges, universities, and other training providers in order for students to pursue learning opportunities, build their skills, and achieve learning credentials.

Best Practice Description

The school system and its component schools have created numerous effective partnerships with other learning institutions to support the learning outcomes of all students. Universities, colleges, technical colleges, trade schools, employment training entities, and other institutions partner with the system and its component schools to help in the education of its students.

The district and its component schools value the participation of other learning and training institutions in the education of its students, and as a result, numerous opportunities to connect learning to the community are evident. The district and its partners have focused on the needs of students and can track and measure the results of the efforts.

The district and its partners have also developed and implemented an effective process of ensuring that the community-at-large understands the opportunities available for partnership and the support of student learning outcomes. The school system has developed a mechanism of continuous data reporting (e.g., dashboards) to allow the community to access the latest data regarding student achievement and system operations.

Use the Best Practice Description to Determine Your Present Performance Level

Practices in Place (Based on the Best Practice Description)

(Continued)

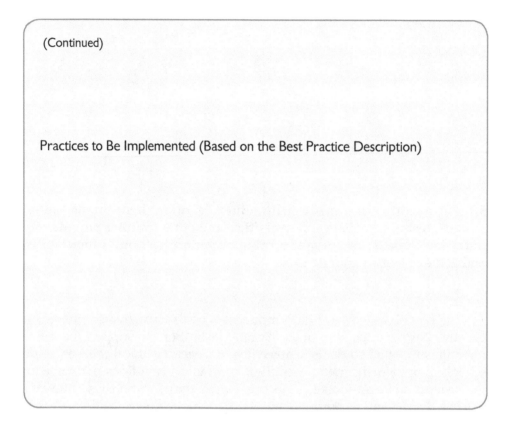

(Continued)

Practices to Be Implemented (Based on the Best Practice Description)

5.3 Opportunities evolve from the school for creating and implementing adult-learning and community development courses to be run within the school building.

Best Practice Description

Adult learning is valued in the school system and individual schools and is seen as a part of the core mission of the district. The leadership of the school system together with community and business partners seeks adult participation in educational programs, with a specific eye toward parents and families of students, and has created substantial opportunities for adult learning through community partnerships. The education of parents and families is seen as a direct conduit to improved academic achievement of students.

The school district, its component schools, and partners develop and maintain services to families that support the learning needs and outcomes of all students. School and community-based learning opportunities for adults are valued and a core component of the school and community culture. The school system and partners have also reached beyond programs to support adult learning to focus on language acquisition and adult literacy among those for whom English is not a first language.

Use the Best Practice Description to Determine Your Present Performance Level

Practices in Place (Based on the Best Practice Description)

Practices to Be Implemented (Based on the Best Practice Description)

10

Taking Action and Measuring Success

Congratulations on making it this far! By now you should have a thorough and working understanding of *Engage Every Family: Five Simple Principles*. But we are not yet finished. At this point, there is a very important question that needs to be asked: So, given this information, what do we do?

What gets measured gets done.

The simple sentence above summarizes the profound implications of engaging every family; by following the five principles you have evidence your efforts have made a difference in the learning lives of students and the degree to which families positively impact that learning.

All of us who have dedicated our lives to educating children have a fundamental understanding of this phrase. We know that if there is measurement, the likelihood of our following through is much greater than if we perceive there to be no measurement or expectation of improvement. Educators have been party to countless initiatives in education that seemingly dissipate into thin air, largely because there was never a real performance expectation or way to measure the improvement. Remember, culture eats change for lunch.

If family engagement is to become a force that improves the learning outcomes of all students, then the degree to which we can plan, execute, and measure our efforts becomes essential. Short of that, we simply have another idea that sounds good, perhaps looks good on paper, and further, has the philosophical support of many, but in the final analysis provides little in shaping more positive outcomes for students.

Let's not let that happen.

Executing strategies that engage every family and have an impact on the learning outcomes of students should be approached with no less attention or vitality than those goals and objectives that are written to produce better results with all students. In a nutshell, family engagement is measurable. Goals and objectives that engage families in the learning lives of their children will produce results if they are well conceived, executed, and measured.

START WITH DATA

Many well-intentioned educators set lofty goals for family engagement. Goals that indicate "more family engagement" or "increase family engagement" may produce little with regard to student achievement. In order to ensure that our efforts in family engagement result in improved learning outcomes for students, we should first look at the data we generate to determine where our finite amount of time, energy, and resources will provide us the best results.

Schools have data. In most cases, more data than they can handle. Most of the time the focus is on data that shows learning trends. Benchmark testing and formative or collaborative assessments usually lead to a high-stakes test upon which principals, teachers, and schools are judged.

It is impossible to list the data that are available in every school. What can be shared here are categories of data. The following chart is an example of the kind of data available in most schools. It is by no means meant to be an all-inclusive list. Feel free to remove those items that are not germane to your school and add those that are.

Let's get started.

This list below is an example of certain kinds of data in schools. It is not comprehensive and may or may not be reflective of the data used in your school. You are encouraged to create a chart that reflects the specific data that is used in your school to promote growth and continuous improvement.

There is no doubt that educators could easily fill this chart, probably more, with the data that is used to promote student achievement and continuous improvement.

To effectively engage every family, it will be important to start with the data that is most important to your school or district. Take the time to complete this chart so that it accurately reflects what is important to your school.

General Student Performance Data	College or Career	Formative	Diagnostic	Summative
Attendance data	SAT	Common formative assessments	Reading diagnostic	Certain types of benchmarks
Absenteeism	ACT	Unit tests	Math diagnostics	Simulated state tests for practice
Discipline data	Career certifications	Spelling/vocabu-lary tests	Language acquisition diagnostic	Required state test
Disproportionality data	Military testing (ASVAB)	Benchmark tests		Any summa-tive test that is required
RTI data	Training completer certificates	Assessments derived from purchased programs that help track growth		
Physical fitness tests	NAEP	Project-based learning assignments		
Graduation rate				
Dropout rate				
Retention rates				
Credit accrual data				

GOAL STATEMENTS

The more broad a goal, the less likely it will be met. The more grandiose a goal, the less likely it will be effective. Here is an example of a goal that might be considered a bit broad and slightly grandiose:

- Every student in the United States will graduate from high school and go to college.

There is no argument that this goal is necessary, but given its broad and grandiose nature, the likelihood of achieving it is fairly slim.

(NCLB might be an example of another goal that simply proved to be impossible to meet.)

The same holds true for family engagement. We tend to compartmentalize family engagement goals separately from learning and school improvement goals. It is common to see family engagement goals that look like this:

- To increase family engagement in our school\district
- To improve parent satisfaction rates with our school\district
- To increase membership in our PTA
- To increase attendance of parents to back-to-school night

What do you think of these goals? Are they manageable? Do you think you will see the results of your labors if you try to implement these goals? Most importantly, how will these goals directly address student performance improvements?

I don't believe that there is a single educator alive who has not heard of or understands the premise of SMART goals. Most everyone in education has become adept at writing SMART goals. However, on the off chance that you have never heard this term, a SMART goal is one that contains a statement which is *specific, measurable, attainable, result oriented,* and *time bound.* There are other versions of the SMART goal, but in essence, this is it. The idea is to ensure that whatever goal we write is specific in its desire to improve, and it is attainable (at least in our lifetime), measurable, and has a finite end. Quite simple, really.

Let's start by going back to our data chart. For purposes of this illustration, we'll pick discipline data. (You should choose whatever data is relevant to your situation.) As we drill through this data, we start to see patterns emerging. Perhaps it is the number and types of students who repeat poor choices and behaviors. Perhaps there are grade-level patterns of discipline issues or maybe a higher rate of disciplinary issues in those grades that are transitions (first year of middle school, etc.).

Whatever the case, review and analyze the data that are available. To further illustrate this example, we'll assume the following is true in the discipline data that we have reviewed:

Grade Level	Infraction	Number of Instances
4th Grade	Bullying	0
5th Grade	Bullying	1
6th Grade	Bullying	9
7th Grade	Bullying	17
8th Grade	Bullying	29

Principle	Rationale
#1 Create a culture that engages every family	
#2 Communicate effectively and build relationships	
#3 Empower every family	
#4 Engage every family in decision making	
#5 Engage the greater community	

Action steps: Record each of the action steps necessary to achieve the goal.

Action Step 1 (Principle #1)

Action Step 2 (Principle #2)

Action Step 3 (Principle #3)

Action Step 4 (Principle #4)

Action Step 5 (Principle #5)

At the end of this chapter, there is a sample goal statement and action-planning chart that will help you examine your data to create SMART goals and action steps to provide measurement to achieve your goals. Use whatever data is important to your school and follow the process outlined in this chapter to connect your improvement goals with family engagement.

It's that simple!

Engage Every Family: Five Simple Principles

School/District Principles Implementation Format Plan

Principle (check one)

_____ A Culture That Engages Every Family   _____ Communicate Effectively and Build Relationships

_____ Engage Every Family in Decision Making   _____ Empower Every Family   _____ Engage the Greater Community

Specific Standard to Be Addressed:

Goal Statement:

Strategy to Be Employed	Who Is Responsible?	What Resources Are Needed?	What Budget Considerations Are There?	Evidence That the Strategy Was Successful (outcome)

Epilogue

Exceeding Expectations

. . . the moment of critical mass, the threshold, the boiling point.

—Malcom Gladwell (from his description
of *The Tipping Point*)

At the onset of this book, I challenged you to take one simple step and begin to embrace the concept of engaging every family in the academic lives of young people. As you worked your way through this book, hopefully you have taken numerous steps to engage every family in order to bring about better learning for their children. If you got this far and you are still enthused or at least intrigued, then the time is now to make the changes necessary to engage every family in your school or district. You will not be sorry.

Consider for a moment that there exists a family somewhere in your school district that very much cares about the success of their children, especially as it relates to school. They want what is best for their child and, as we have learned, they seek the opportunity for their children to exceed them in their quality of life. For generations, parents have desired this simple goal, and for many generations, it has come true.

Our society and economy are changing dramatically. For the first time in anyone's memory, our children may not (and in some cases cannot) exceed us in their quality of life. It is this very notion that strikes fear in many families, and it is because of this notion that we must engage every family.

Family engagement is not optional. It is not an idea that can sit on a shelf until we determine we have the time or interest. It should not be relegated to the end of the list of important reforms we must enact.

We are spending a great deal of time, energy, and resources on learning all we can about twenty-first century instruction. We spend millions of professional development dollars searching for those ideas that will bring us success with every student—a success that still eludes us. In all of this, the notion of family engagement, that being empowering the first and most influential teachers of children, seems to somehow get lost. We simply cannot let that continue to happen.

And so, you have a decision to make. Will you consider the ideas in this book? Will you truthfully examine your beliefs and values and determine what you think about this whole idea of family engagement? Will you work toward a permanent change in the culture of your school, a change that has at its nucleus the belief that families can be a powerful force in helping us succeed with our students? Will you confront whatever fears you may have about families and work to eliminate them? Will you embrace the simple idea that in order to be successful with every student we must engage every family? Will you help others do the same?

TWO HUGE QUESTIONS

While you are thinking about the questions above, let me try and put it another way. Let's limit the questions to two—but two really big, really important questions.

In just about every workshop, I get to a point where I try to support and justify the need to understand the importance of family engagement and what it will take to be successful with every family. You will recall that in Chapter 1 I told the story of *Yagottawanna*. The premise of *Yagottawanna* is simple; your personal desire to make a difficult change (or choice or decision) starts with the very simple notion that the change (choice, decision) is something we desire. If it isn't, then the likelihood of success isn't very high.

So to encapsulate this idea, let me now ask you two very important questions. The questions might seem simple, but after a few moments of consideration, they could easily become more daunting. There is space below to provide answers or to jot notes about your answers to each question.

Question 1: What do you want?

For purposes of this exercise, limit your thinking to your professional career as an educator or, if you are still in school or just starting out, think about what a satisfying career in education would look like. What do you want as an educator?

What did you write? Did you write about your personal and professional satisfaction? Did you write about being happy in your chosen field? Did you list specific items like "all children will be successful in my classroom?" Did you state your responses in the form of what you did not want, that is, "I don't want students who misbehave." The beauty of this question is that there are no wrong answers. Whatever you think . . . is exactly right. Now let's move to question number two.

Question 2: Considering your response(s) to Question 1, what are you willing to do to get what you want?

Regardless of what you wrote as responses to Question 1, you now have to determine what you are willing to do to get that which you said you wanted. So what are you willing to do either personally or professionally to attain what you believe is important to you?

(Continued)

(Continued)

Only you can answer these questions. But here is what I know: Every educator with whom I have had the privilege of coming in contact wants to be successful. They gravitate toward those ideas that are proven to be successful, and they work incredibly hard at helping every one of their students learn. I see evidence of this every day. It is this belief that encourages me to be hopeful that more and more educators will embrace the important concept of family engagement.

If you follow the processes outlined in this book, embrace the philosophy, believe that every family desperately wants to be engaged but may not know how or have the opportunity to do so, and believe that family engagement leads to student success, then you will hit the critical mass . . . the tipping point of family engagement.

What did we do in school today? We learned that the power of family engagement will change the trajectory of school improvement. We learned that with an examination of our values and beliefs and a simple process, we can truly begin to engage every family and leverage success for every student . . . *every* student.

And yes, there is homework.

References

Adger, C., & Locke, J. (2000). *Broadening the base: School/community partnerships serving language minority students at risk.* (Educational Practice Rep. No. 6). Santa Cruz, CA: Center for Research on Education, Diversity and Excellence.

Baker, A. J. (2000). Making the promise of parent involvement a reality. *The High School Magazine, 7*(15), 15–17.

Bandura, A. (1997). *Self-efficacy: The exercise of control.* New York: Freeman.

Bauch, J. P. (1989). The transparent school model. *Educational Leadership, 47*(2), 32–34.

Bauch, P. A., & Goldring, E. B. (1995). Parent involvement and school responsiveness: Facilitating the home-school connection in schools of choice. *Educational Evaluation and Policy Analysis, 17*(1), 1–21.

Blank, M., Melaville, A., & Shah, B. P. (2003). *Making the difference: Research and practice in community schools.* Washington, DC: Coalition for Community Schools. Retrieved from http://www.communityschools.org/CCSFullReport.pdf

Bolman, L. G., & Deal, T. E. (2002). *Reframing the path to school leadership.* Thousand Oaks, CA: Corwin.

Boyd, V. (1992). *School context: Bridge or barrier to change.* Southwest Educational Development Laboratory. Retrieved from http://www.sedl.org/change/school

Brinckerhoff, J., & Vincent, L. (1986). Increasing parental decision-making at their child's individualized educational program meeting. *Journal of the Division for Early Childhood, 11*(1), 46–58.

Bryk, A. S., & Schneider, B. (2002). *Trust in schools: A core resource for improvement.* New York, NY: Russell Sage Foundation.

Caplan, J. G. (2000). *Building strong family-school partnerships to support high student achievement.* The Informed Educators Series. Arlington, VA: Educational Research Service.

Christenson, S. L., & Sheridan, S. M. (2001). *School and families: Creating essential connections for learning.* New York: The Guilford Press.

Commissioner's Parent Advisory Council. (2007). *The missing piece of the proficiency puzzle.* (Final Report to the Kentucky Department of Education). Pritchard Committee for Academic Excellence.

Constantino, S. M. (2003). *Engaging all families: Creating a positive school culture by putting research into practice.* Lanham, MD: Rowman and Littlefield.

Crozier, G., & Davies J. (2007). Hard to reach parents or hard to reach schools? A discussion of home-school relations, with particular reference to Bangladeshi and Pakistani parents. *British Educational Research Journal, 33*(3), 295–313.

Cullingford, C., & Morrison, M. (1999). Relationships between parents and schools: A case study. *Educational Review, 51*(3), 1, 253-262.

Deal, T. E. (1993). The culture of schools. In M. Sashkin & H. J. Walberg (Eds.), *Educational leadership and school culture.* Berkeley, California: McCutchan Publishing.

Deal, T. E., & Peterson, K. D. (1990). *The principal's role in shaping school culture.* Washington, DC: Office of Educational Research and Improvement.

Deal, T. E., & Peterson, K. D. (1994). *The leadership paradox: Balancing logic and artistry in schools.* San Francisco: Jossey-Bass.

Deal, T. E., & Peterson, K. D. (1999). *Shaping school culture: The heart of leadership.* San Francisco: Jossey-Bass.

Decker, L .E., & Decker, V. A., Boo, M. R., Gregg, G. A., Erickson, J., (2001). *Engaging families and communities: Pathways to educational success.* Fairfax, VA: National Community Education Association.

DeLaney, R. (1997, March). *Parent participation in educational decision making: A high stakes procedure.* Paper presented at the annual meeting of the American Educational Research Association, Chicago, IL.

Derubetis, D., & Yanok, J. (1989). Comparative study of parental participation in regular and special education programs. *Exceptional children, 56,* 195–200.

Deslandes, R., Royer, E., Potvisn P., & Leclere, D. (1999). Patterns of home and school partnership for general and special education students at the secondary level. *Exceptional Children, 65,* 496–506.

Drake, D. D. (2000). Parents and families as partners in the education process: Collaboration for the success of students in public schools. *ERS Spectrum,* 34–35.

Eccles, J. S., & Harold, R. D. (1994, November). *Family involvement in children's and adolescents' schooling,* in *Family-school links: How do they affect educational outcomes?* Symposium conducted at Pennsylvania State University.

Effective Schools. (2015). *About us.* Retrieved from www.effectiveschools.com/about-us

Epstein, J. L., & Becker, H. J. (1982). Teacher practices of parent involvement: Problems and possibilities. *Elementary School Journal, 83,* 103–113.

Epstein, J. L., & Salinas, K. C. (2004). Partnering with families and communities. *Educational Leadership, 61*(8), 12–18.

Epstein, J. L., Salinas, K. C., Jackson, V. E., and educators in Baltimore City Public School System. (1995). *TIPS (Teachers Involve Parents in Schoolwork) manual for teachers: Language arts, science/health, and math interactive homework in the middle grades.* Baltimore, MD: Center on School, Family, and Community Partnerships, Johns Hopkins University.

Epstein, J. L., & Sanders, M. G. (2006) Prospects for change: Preparing educators for school, family, and community partnerships. *Peabody Journal of Education, 81*(2), 81–120.

Epstein, J. L., Sanders, M. G., Sheldon, S. B., Simon, B. S., Salinas, K. C., Jansorn, N. R., . . . Williams, K. J. (2009). *School, family, and community partnerships: Your handbook for action.* (3rd ed.). Thousand Oaks, CA: Corwin.

Epstein, J., Sanders, M., Simon, B., Salinas, K., Jansorn, N., and Voorhis, F. (2002). *School, family and community partnerships: Your handbook for action.* Thousand Oaks, CA: Corwin.

Epstein, J. L., & Sheldon, S. B. (2002). Present and accounted for: Improving student attendance through family and community involvement. *Journal of Educational Research, 95*, 308–318.

Espinosa, L. M. (1995). *Hispanic parent involvement in early childhood programs*. ERIC Clearinghouse on Elementary and Early Childhood Education. Retrieved from ERICDigests.org (ED382412).

Finders, M., & Lewis, C. (1994). Why some parents don't come to school. *Educating for Diversity, 51*(8), 50–54.

Flanagan, A., & Grissmer, D. (2002). The role of federal resources in closing the achievement gap. In J. E. Chubb & T. Loveless (Eds.), *Bridging the achievement gap* (pp. 199–225). Washington DC: Brookings Institute.

Fullan, M. (2001). *Leading in a culture of change*. San Francisco, CA: Jossey-Bass.

Geertz, C. (1973). *The interpretation of cultures*. New York, NY: Basic Books.

Glenn, H. S., & Nelsen, J. (1988). *Raising self-reliant children in a self-indulgent world*. Roseville, CA: Prima Publishing.

Gonder, P. O. (1994). *Improving school climate & culture*. In D. L. Hymes (Ed.), AASA Critical Issues Series. Retrieved from http://files.eric.ed.gov/fulltext/ED371485.pdf

Gretz, P. (2003). School and community partnerships: Cultivating friends [High school ed.] *Principal Leadership, 3*, 32–40.

Hallgarten, J. (2000) *Parents exist, ok!?* Great Britian: Biddles.

Harris, A. (2009). *Distributed leadership: Different perspectives*. Amsterdam: Springer.

Harvard Family Research Project. (2013). *Tips for administrators, teachers, and families: How to share data effectively*. Cambridge, MA: Harvard Family Research Project. Retrieved from http://www.hfrp.org/publications-resources/browse-our-publications/tips-for-administrators-teachers-and-families-how-to-share-data-effectively

Haviland, W. A. (1975). *Cultural anthropology* (3rd. ed.). New York, NY: Holt, Rhinehart & Winston.

Havinghurst R. J. (1972). *Developmental tasks and education*. New York, NY: McKay.

Henderson, A. T., Mapp, K. L., Johnson, V. R., & Davies, D. (2007). *Beyond the bake sale: The essential guide to family-school partnerships*. New York, NY: The New Press.

Hoover-Dempsey, K. V., & Sandler, H. (1997). Why do parents become involved in their children's education? *Review of Educational Research, 67*(1), 3–42.

Hoover-Dempsey, K. V., Walker, J. M. T., & Sandler, H. M. (2005). Parents' motivations for involvement in their children's education. In E. N. Patrikakou, R. P. Weisberg, S. Redding, & H. J. Walberg (Eds.), *School-Family Partnerships for Children's Success* (pp. 40–56). New York, NY: Teachers College Press.

Hornby, G. (2011). Barriers to parent involvement in education: An exploratory model. *Educational Review, 63*(1), 37–52.

Kania, J., & Kramer, M. (2011, Winter). Collective impact. *Stanford Social Innovation Review*.

Kena, G., Aud, S., Johnson, F., Wang, X., Zhang, J., Rathbun, A., . . . Kristapovich, P. (2014). *The condition of education 2014* (NCES 2014-083). U.S. Department of Education, National Center for Education Statistics. Washington, DC. Retrieved from http://nces.ed.gov/pubsearch

Kotter, J. P., & Cohen, D. S. (2002). *The heart of change*. Boston, MA: Harvard Business School Press.

Kretzmann, J. P., & McKnight, J. L. (1993). *Building communities from the inside out: A path toward finding and mobilizing a community's assets.* Evanston, IL: Institute for Policy Research.

Lake Forest College. (2010). *History of the effective schools movement.* Retrieved from https://www.lakeforest.edu/library/archives/effective-schools/HistoryofEffectiveSchools.php

Lareau, A. (1987). Social class differences in family-school relationships: The importance of cultural capital. *Sociology of Education, 60,* 73–85.

Liontos, L. (1992). *At-risk families and schools becoming partners.* ERIC Clearinghouse of Educational Management. Retrieved from EricDIGEST (ED242055).

Malen, B., & Ogawa, R. T. (1988). Professional-patron influence on site-based governance councils: A confounding case study. *Educational Evaluation and Policy Analysis, 10,* 251–270.

Mapp, K. L. (2003). Having their say: Parents describe why and how they are engaged in their children's learning. *The School-Community Journal, 13*(1), 35–64.

Mapp, K. L., & Kuttner, P. J. (2013). *Partners in education: A dual capacity-building framework for building family school partnerships.* Austin, TX: SEDL.

Markow, D., Macia, L., & Lee, H. (2013). *The Metlife survey of the American teacher: Challenges for school leaders.* New York, NY: Metlife.

McBride, B. (1991). Preservice teachers' attitudes toward parental involvement. *Teacher Education Quarterly, 18,* 59–67.

National Network of Partnership Schools. (n.d.). *Epstein's six types of parent involvement.* Retrieved from http://www.csos.jhu.edu/p2000/sixtypes.htm

National PTA. (2000). *Building successful partnerships.* Bloomington, IN: National Education Service.

Parsons, B. A., & Schmitz, C. C. (1999). *Everything you wanted to know about logic models but were afraid to ask.* Paper presented at the annual meeting of the American Evaluation Association, Orlando, FL.

Patterson, J. L., Purkey, S. C., & Parker, J. V. (1986). *Productive school systems for a nonrational world.* Alexandria, VA: Association for Supervision and Curriculum Development.

Patterson, K., Grenny, J., McMillan, R., & Switzler, A. (2012). *Crucial conversations: Tools for talking when stakes are high* (2nd ed.). New York, NY: McGraw Hill.

Pew Research Center. (2015). *Mobile technology fact sheet.* Retrieved from http://www.pewinternet.org

Phi Delta Kappa International. (2014). *46th annual PDK/Gallup poll of the public's attitudes toward the public schools.* Retrieved from http://pdkintl.org/programs-resources/poll/

Pink, D. (2009). *Drive: The surprising truth about what motivates us.* New York, NY: Riverhead.

Price, H. B. (2008). *Mobilizing the community to help students succeed.* Alexandria, VA: ASCD.

Pritchard Committee for Academic Excellence. (2015). *About the Governor's Commonwealth Institute for Parent Leadership.* Retrieved from http://www.prichardcommittee.org/our-initiatives/gcipl

Rodriguez, R. J., Blatz, E. T., & Elbaum B. (2014). Parents' views of schools' involvement efforts. *Exceptional Children, 81*(1), 79–95.

Sanders, M. G., & Harvey, A. (2002). Beyond the school walls: A case study of principal leadership for school-community collaboration. *Teachers College Record, 104*(7), 1345–1368.

Schein, E. H. (2010). *Organizational culture and leadership* (4th ed.). San Francisco, CA: Jossey-Bass.

Shepard, R. N. (1990). *Mind sights: Original visual illusions, ambiguities, and other anomalies, with a commentary on the play of mind in perception and art.* New York, NY: W. H. Freeman and Co.

Sims, S. J., & Sims, R. R. (2004). *Managing school system change: Charting a course for renewal.* Greenwich, CT: Information Age Publishing.

Smrekar, C., & Cohen-Vogel, L. (2001). The voices of parents: Rethinking the intersection of family and school. *Peabody Journal of Education, 76*(2), 75–100.

Stilwell, A., & Ferguson, D. (n.d.). [*Did you know...*] *About four ways to increase parental efficacy?* National Institute for Urban School Improvement. Retrieved from http://www.niusi.org/pdf/parent_efficacy.pdf?v_document_name=Increase%20Parental%20Efficacy

Stolp, S., & Smith, S. C. (1994, January). School culture and climate: The role of the leader. *OSSC Bulletin.* Eugene, OR: Oregon School Study Council.

Tiland, R. (2014, June). The power of video—The premier communications tool of today. *Forbes.* Retrieved from http://www.forbes.com/sites/womensmedia/2014/06/22/the-power-of-video-the-premier-communications-tool-of-today/

Wagner, C. (2004/2005). Leadership for an improved school culture: How to assess and improve the culture of your school. *Kentucky School Leader,* 10–16.

Waller, W. (1932). *The sociology of teaching.* New York, NY: Wiley.

Wehlage, G., Smith, G., & Lipman, P. (1992, Spring). Restructuring urban schools: The New Futures experience. *American Educational Research Journal, 29*(1), 51–93.

Index

CORWIN A SAGE Company

CORWIN HAS ONE MISSION: to enhance education through intentional professional learning.

We build long-term relationships with our authors, educators, clients, and associations who partner with us to develop and continuously improve the best evidence-based practices that establish and support lifelong learning.

Solutions you want. Experts you trust. Results you need.

Author Consulting

AUTHOR CONSULTING

On-site professional learning with sustainable results! Let us help you design a professional learning plan to meet the unique needs of your school or district. www.corwin.com/pd

Institutes

INSTITUTES

Corwin Institutes provide collaborative learning experiences that equip your team with tools and action plans ready for immediate implementation. www.corwin.com/institutes

eCourses

ECOURSES

Practical, flexible online professional learning designed to let you go at your own pace. www.corwin.com/ecourses

Read2Earn

READ2EARN

Did you know you can earn graduate credit for reading this book? Find out how: www.corwin.com/read2earn

Contact an account manager at (800) 831-6640 or visit **www.corwin.com** for more information.